MONUMENT

Emily Sheehan

CURRENCY PRESS
The performing arts publisher

RED
STITCH

THE
ACTORS'
THEATRE

CURRENT THEATRE SERIES

First published in 2023
by Currency Press
Gadigal Land, PO Box 2287 Strawberry Hills, NSW, 2012, Australia
enquiries@currency.com.au
www.currency.com.au

in association with Red Stitch

Typeset by Brighton Gray for Currency Press.
Cover image by Robert Blackburn & Work Art Life Studios.
Cover shows **Sarah Sutherland and Julia Hanna.**
Cover design by Mathias Johansson for Currency Press.

Currency Press acknowledges the Traditional Owners of the Country on which we live and work. We pay our respects to all Aboriginal and Torres Strait Islander Elders, past and present.

A catalogue record for this book is available from the National Library of Australia

Contents

Currency Press acknowledges the Traditional Owners of the Country on which we live and work. We pay our respects to all Aboriginal and Torres Strait Islander Elders, past and present.

For my mother, Maureen Sheehan, who taught me the power of red lipstick and joining the union.

Monument was first produced by Red Stitch Actors' Theatre at the Red Stitch Theatre, St Kilda, on the lands of the Boon Wurrung and Wurundjeri Woi Wurrung peoples of the Kulin Nation, on 9 August 2023, with the following cast:

EDITH	Sarah Sutherland
ROSIE	Julia Hanna

Director, Ella Caldwell
Set and Costume Designer, Sophie Woodward
Lighting Designer, Amelia Lever-Davidson
Sound Designer, Danni A. Eposito
Assistant Director, Ibrahim Halaçoglu
Stage Manager, Rain Iyahen
Assistant Stage Manager, Eliza Stone
Makeup Advisor, Harriet O'Donnell
VCA Set and Costume Design Intern, Filipe Filihia

Monument was developed through Red Stitch's INK writing program.

Acknowledgements

This play has benefitted hugely from the creative input of an incredible artistic team at Red Stitch Actors' Theatre. My heartfelt thanks to Ella Caldwell, Joanna Murray-Smith and Bridget Balodis for their intellectual rigour and enormous patience in the dramaturgical wrangling of this play.

Thank you to Laura Tingle for her advice and instincts on multiple facets of Edith's character and backstory, and for answering my many questions about the political dimensions of the narrative.

Thank you to Sarah Sutherland, Tahlee Fereday and Julia Hanna. It has been a pleasure and privilege to develop these characters with you.

I'd like to thank my friends Maddie Nunn, Keziah Warner and Jamaica Zuanetti for two and a half years of encouragement, conversation and artistic input. Your friendship and dramaturgical minds have been crucial.

Thank you also to Melbourne Theatre Company and the early support of Jennifer Medway, Chris Mead and Rachel Chant through the Cybec development program.

And to my husband, Tomas Van Wyk, for your unwavering support.

Introduction

We don't like to admit it, but women—and the way we think about them—in politics, remain in uncomfortable terrain.

That is certainly the case in Australia. And it certainly seems to be the case in the rest of the Anglo-sphere. Think Jacinda Ardern, Hilary Clinton or Liz Truss—whatever their particular levels of political competence.

We like to think there has been much progress, both in the strides women have taken to be brought into the political tent of the federal parliament, and in the way we talk about issues that particularly affect us. A decade ago, the trauma of Julia Gillard's prime ministership which—whatever its achievements—seemed often to be drowning in the attacks on her, gave cause for pause about those optimistic presumptions.

It seems we are still coming to terms with the treatment of Gillard. A 2023 play dedicated twenty minutes just to the recreation of her famous speech about misogyny.

But beyond that, there is the pragmatic reality that the way we contemplate, or even agonise over, the treatment of women in politics seems a million light years from the issues facing so many women in their daily lives.

Enter Emily Sheehan's compelling study of two very contemporary women: Edith—unexpectedly so close to the leadership of her country—and Rosie—one of life's pragmatic observers and do-ers.

Their unplanned encounter challenges them both, reveals much about what we take for granted in politics, about the power of family and of love, and takes us into the decisions and compromises we all make about what we do with our lives.

Laura Tingle,
Canberra 2023

CHARACTERS

EDITH, female, 38, a world leader

ROSIE, female, 22, the makeup girl

LOCATION

The presidential suite of a heritage listed hotel.

TIME

The play runs as one closed-time closed-place continuous scene.

A NOTE ON PUNCTUATION

… indicates the character is choosing not to speak and should be afforded this space.

— indicates a character's speech is cut off.

/ indicates the exact point of interruption in overlapping dialogue.

Beat is shorter than a pause.

{Time} in brace brackets marks dialogue to be adjusted for the production runtime, e.g. '{Thirty-minute} call.'

{Makeup step} in brace brackets marks dialogue to be adjusted for the step Rosie is up to, e.g. 'So long as I can keep {blending}.'

Non-intrusive makeup instructions from Rosie to Edith are encouraged when needed to keep the actor safe, e.g. 'Close your eyes', 'Look down', 'Hold there', 'Hold your breath'.

This play was written with Australian specificity. However, I encourage tweaks to the text to situate the play in the context in which it is presented.

The presidential suite of a heritage listed hotel. 5:30 a.m.

The room is empty, though the light and sound from the adjoining suite suggests someone is showering.

A row of transparent garment bags hang on a freestanding rack.

A knock on the door. After a moment, the unmistakable buzz of a swipe card unlocks the door.

ROSIE: [*offstage, to security*] Thank you!

> ROSIE *enters, tray of coffees in one hand, wheeling her makeup kit behind her.*

[*Calling out*] Morning! Sorry I'm a few …

> ROSIE *finds a place to set the coffees down.*

Ms Aldridge?

> ROSIE *knocks on the door to the adjoining suite. No answer.*

It's Rosie. It's five thirty-six.
Are you nearly ready?
But take your time! Obviously.
I'll just be setting up.

> ROSIE *begins setting up her makeup kit, but her attention is soon drawn to the garment bags.*
>
> *She finds a moment to straighten them. She unzips one to reveal a pink Chanel dress.*

> ROSIE *takes the Chanel out of the bag, admires it, holds it against her body as if to imagine wearing it.*
>
> *She knows she shouldn't, but she slides her phone out of her pocket to snap a quick selfie with the dress.*
>
> *She can't get the right light, so she throws open the curtains and poses by the window.*
>
> *She raises her phone high to capture a selfie, without seeing the door to the adjoining suite open.*
>
> EDITH *enters. Fresh from the shower. Completely naked.*

> EDITH *sees* ROSIE.

> EDITH *screams. This makes* ROSIE *scream.*

EDITH: AHHH/HHHH!
ROSIE: SORRY! I DIDN'T KNOW YOU WERE READY!

> EDITH *rushes back inside the suite and slams the door.*

> ROSIE *races to put the dress back.*

[*Calling out*] Security swiped me in! I'm here to get you in glam and out the door for—

> EDITH *re-enters in a robe, wet hair, no makeup, puffy eyes.*

EDITH: What the flying fuck are you doing sneaking into my hotel room! How dare you just enter without even knocking!
ROSIE: I did!
EDITH: Don't you know that people like me live in constant fear of deranged killers and pervert kidnappers and unhinged vigilantes sneaking into our hotels after releasing some alt-right manifesto online!
ROSIE: I'm not any of those things!
EDITH: What if my security detail came in and shot you after hearing me scream?!
ROSIE: That could happen?!
EDITH: And WHY are the curtains open?!
ROSIE: I'll close them.

> ROSIE *moves swiftly to close the curtains.*

EDITH: You thought it would be appropriate to OPEN the curtains before I'm even dressed for the day?!
ROSIE: I'll wait outside until you're ready.
EDITH: Stop! I'm just thrown.
ROSIE: I know.
EDITH: You scared me.
ROSIE: You scared me.
EDITH: Tasha's usually here playing pointguard.
ROSIE: Yes! Tasha. She blew up my DMs this morning.
EDITH: My team is—
ROSIE: I heard.

EDITH: Travel nightmare.

ROSIE: Too much fog or something?

EDITH: A diverted flight, but they'll make it in time for the ceremony. Which is what matters.

ROSIE: You were lucky.

EDITH: Family stuff. Flew in last night. They need me downstairs to meet my driver in ninety minutes.

ROSIE: That's not much time.

EDITH: By the schedule we're an hour behind. [*Reading the schedule*] Downstairs seven a.m. Arrivals from eight a.m. My people will all be there, waiting for me. Ceremony begins at nine. Get the paperwork signed and out of the way. Then—this is where you come in—official photography outside on the lawns, so I'll need touch-ups.

ROSIE: Got it.

EDITH: Then my big moment. Full pomp and ceremony. After that, a number of formal functions. For that we'll do full face, different dress, your call on hair.

ROSIE: Full glam. Done.

EDITH: This is going to be a really big year for me.

ROSIE: You mean day?

EDITH: No, I mean year.

ROSIE: Great! I'll get set up. So you'll just be … ? [*Gesturing to* EDITH *texting on her phone*] Yep! You stay there. Allergic to anything?

EDITH: No.

ROSIE: Any long-term skin conditions, scalp irritations, skin sensitivities, redness or itchiness after using makeup?

EDITH: No.

ROSIE: Aversion to fragrance?

EDITH: No.

ROSIE: How much makeup do you usually wear?

EDITH: A normal amount? More these days.

ROSIE: We don't want to overdo it. Unless that's what you usually do?

EDITH: I mean, I want to look good.

ROSIE: You look good right now.

EDITH: Just be honest and tell me I look awful.

ROSIE: *Well.*

EDITH: Exactly.

ROSIE: You're actually pretty clammy, but I can help with that.

EDITH: You gave me a fright.

ROSIE: Do you get this way when you're nervous?

EDITH: No.

ROSIE: It's a non-judgemental space here.

EDITH: It's actually my space we're in and it's not for you to judge how judgemental it is.

ROSIE: I just need to know if you're clammy because of nerves, or if you're generally quite a sweaty person? In which case you'll need a strong antiperspirant.

EDITH: It's not nerves.

EDITH *grabs one of the coffees and takes a sip.*

[*Recoiling from the taste*] Ugh! There's milk in this.

ROSIE: Vanilla latte.

EDITH: I take a double espresso.

ROSIE: That'd be my coffee you're drinking.

EDITH: [*relieved*] Right! [*Switching coffees*] So this one is—?

ROSIE: That's also a vanilla latte.

EDITH: … Is that a joke?

ROSIE: I was up all night. I needed two. I didn't realise I was supposed to …

Pause.

Take mine! Drink both, even.

EDITH: Milk makes me feel off in the morning.

Pause.

ROSIE: No-one mentioned anything about getting coffee.

Pause.

EDITH: Well this is a bit of a weird moment between us, isn't it?

ROSIE: I'll get some sent up. Oh! Reception asked if you're ready for breakfast. Have you eaten?

EDITH: Not since last night.

ROSIE: Should I tell them to send it up?

EDITH: I hate the menu here.

ROSIE *picks up the hotel phone, dials '2' for housekeeping.*

ROSIE: [*on the hotel phone*] Can I get a pot of black coffee sent up? … No milk … The newspapers? Great! [*Hanging up. To* EDITH] It's on its way. [*Beat*] You stay here a lot?

EDITH: My father did. He liked the staff. They always wanted photos. I find it, *you know*.

ROSIE: No?

EDITH: Overt.

ROSIE: Totally! I knew it'd be nice, but this place is extra. Shall we start on skin prep?

> EDITH *accepts and takes a seat in the makeup chair.*
>
> *Skin prep takes a few minutes. During the following,* ROSIE *spritzes* EDITH*'s face with flower essence. Smoothes serum into her skin. Gently massages moisturiser into her face, using the warmth of her hands to help it absorb. Applies lip balm.*

EDITH: The entire building is heritage listed. The carpet, the wallpaper, even the doorknobs, would you believe? If anything is damaged they have to make every effort to restore it to its original condition. That or recreate it in its original image.

ROSIE: What, just keep swapping it out for more of the same?

EDITH: More or less.

> *Edith's phone gets a string of notifications.*
>
> ROSIE *continues assessing Edith's complexion and selects the appropriate products.*

[*Reading the notification*] What a colossal hogfucker.

ROSIE: What is it?

EDITH: The self-appointed sheriffs of the internet. [*While completing each step*] Screenshot rape and or death threat. Forward to the authorities. Block. Move on.

ROSIE: I'm sure you're after the perfect canvas today. Normal, dry, oily, combination, sensitive?

EDITH: Normal.

ROSIE: [*not agreeing*] Hmm.

EDITH: What?

ROSIE: Are you sure?

EDITH: Yes.

ROSIE: Dull, rough complexion, slightly inflamed, red patches, some visible lines. Does your skin feel tight since getting out of the shower?

EDITH: Yes.

ROSIE: You're dry.

EDITH: Excuse you?

ROSIE: Don't want you looking splotchy.

EDITH: Splotchy?

ROSIE: Foundation clings to dead skin cells. The base will look uneven if you're not properly hydrated. Here, try the Baume 27. [*Passing her a jar of moisturiser from her kit*] It's a total dupe for the Crème de la Mer.

EDITH: Right.

ROSIE: It's still super-expensive though. I wouldn't share this with just *anyone*. But obviously you can use as much as you like.

EDITH: [*examining the jar*] Thanks for the tip.

> *Pause.*

ROSIE: [*stopping herself before applying a product*] Oh. [*Looking from another angle*]. Oh dear. [*Face-to-face*] Hmm.

EDITH: What's wrong?

ROSIE: You sleep on your face.

EDITH: *Excuse you?*

ROSIE: I can tell from how puffy your eyes are. They're quite dark circles.

EDITH: I'm usually fueled by caffeine.

ROSIE: I'll need to factor in ten minutes for colour-correcting.

EDITH: I'm running on two and a half hours' sleep.

ROSIE: You're as bad as me. Crazy boyfriend dramas and all that. You?

EDITH: Twitter shitstorm.

ROSIE: You're surprisingly congested for such a dry canvas. How many steps in your skincare routine?

> EDITH *ignores her. She's busy with something on her phone.*

Please tell me it's at least five.

> EDITH *ignores her.*

Do you at least *take off* your makeup at night?

> EDITH *ignores her.*

Fine, chat me through what steps you usually take, and I can work backwards from there.

EDITH: When I get home at night, usually around midnight, my assistant dumps my things in the foyer while I take off my heels, stockings and bra and reheat whatever takeaway Adam ordered. I pour a chardy and eat on the couch and try not to drop any bites of spring roll on my laptop. I take two hours to get through emails. Check the international headlines. I take my one uninterrupted shit of the day, pop a zopiclone, and then crawl into bed with Adam. If he wakes up and I'm feeling generous, I'll give him half a handjob—he usually finishes it himself—and pass out on the pillow once my sleeping pills kick in. That's my skincare routine.

ROSIE: Wow. I'm really sorry about the coffee.

Edith's phone rings. It's Tasha.

EDITH: [*taking the call*] Tasha! Did you see the coverage this morning? [*Thrilled*] Killer! Eight front pages; six kind, two not so kind. Ten or so editorials across those with *overwhelmingly positive* tones. One disgusting cartoon. Lots of the C-word on twitter. A huge amount of support on Facebook and Instagram. That's locally. I also have nine international cover stories. Spring cover for *Vogue*.

EDITH *gets another call. It's Adam.*

[*To Tasha*] I'm getting a call from Adam … I-will-I-will-I-will. [*Taking the call from Adam*] Adam! Just out of the shower now … This is deteriorating faster than I can lower my standards … No I haven't seen— [*Looking around*] Oh! They're on the bench.

EDITH *points to* ROSIE *to indicate she should bring her the folders.* ROSIE *does.*

Yes yes yes. [*Opening one up and flicking through the pages*] Ah, briefing papers, press clippings, schedule, talking points, guest list, look book … Oh! Did you see this one [*Reading a headline*] 'The First Couple's secret to a modern marriage.' People are really rooting for us … I know … I KNOW! … You're taking off? Finally! Call me the minute you can switch back on.

EDITH *hangs up the phone.*

Pause.

The plane's finally taking off. They're a bit late … But that's fine … I'll just be here … Alone … It's not like it's my hour of need or anything.

ROSIE: You're not alone.

> ROSIE *mists her face with floral essence.*

EDITH: Remind me how Tasha found you?

ROSIE: I did her face for the fundraiser.

EDITH: We go to a lot of fundraisers.

ROSIE: She showed up at my beauty counter. Said she got a last-minute invite. And I had twenty minutes to make her look amazing.

EDITH: *You did that?* I do remember that! Her cheekbones!

ROSIE: It was the contouring. She ignores her bone structure, but it's her X-factor.

EDITH: She really did look amazing.

ROSIE: Give the serums a minute to settle in.

> *Silence as* ROSIE *continues skin prep.*

EDITH: [*intrigued*] What's my X-factor?

ROSIE: Your eyes. They're very human.

> EDITH *smiles.*

EDITH: Your reputation precedes you.

ROSIE: I literally died when she called me.

EDITH: My usual girl's stuck on the plane and the resident hair-and-makeup artist here is older than this heritage hotel.

ROSIE: This is unreal. Painting your face after seeing it on telly every night. 'I'm Edith Aldridge. That's our show for this evening. Goodnight.'

EDITH: You missed the emphasis: 'Good*night*'. [*Beat*] Well if that's what you can do in twenty, imagine what you can pull off in an hour.

ROSIE: And you have my full attention. No high-maintenance loyalty-card holders and their cashed-up hubbies wearing 'Sex Pest' by Tom Ford.

EDITH: What?

ROSIE: David Jones.

EDITH: What about it?

ROSIE: It's where I work.

EDITH: You aren't a professional makeup artist?

ROSIE: I was freelance, but weekends are time for me and my boyfriend now, you know?

EDITH: … Right.

Unimpressed, EDITH *takes out a magazine from her folder.*

Can you make me look like this?

ROSIE *holds up the magazine, Edith's face fills the front cover.*

ROSIE: [*reading*] 'Edith Aldridge: A Modern Icon.' You look hot. Is there a saucy, political tell-all in here?

EDITH: Only the 'What's in your handbag?' variety.

ROSIE: Stop. What's in your handbag says so much about a woman.

EDITH: It says nothing about a woman.

ROSIE: Mmm-hmm, it says way more than people realise.

EDITH: What the beauty industrial complex thinks is beautiful.

ROSIE: Makeup isn't about being beautiful anymore, it's about being interesting.

EDITH: [*intrigued*] Huh.

ROSIE: So Edith. What's in your handbag?

EDITH: I actually have no idea.

ROSIE: What do you mean?

EDITH: Someone would have signed off on something my team put together.

ROSIE: Did they use any of your own products?

EDITH: Not likely.

ROSIE: Then what's the point?

EDITH: Optics. [*Beat*] I want you to copy that exact look for today.

ROSIE: That's the wrong lip colour for you. You need something loud.

EDITH: I don't do 'loud'.

ROSIE: It's holding you back.

EDITH: I prefer a nude lip.

ROSIE: You look washed out.

EDITH: That's my skintone.

ROSIE: They matched it wrong.

ROSIE *finds a lipstick in her kit.*

[*Handing her the lipstick*] Here, *this* would be the perfect nude for you.

EDITH: [*reading the label*] Dior Stone Fruit.

ROSIE: Trust me.

EDITH: And how are you so sure?

ROSIE *zips her lips.*

What? Tell me.

ROSIE: It's the exact same colour as your nips. If you match your lips to your nips, it's guaranteed the perfect nude. It'll give contrast, while still blending into your natural hues. [*Pointing to the magazine*] See that? That's a dusty rose. Actually, it's more of a sandy beige. But you? You are a stone fruit.

EDITH *holds up the lipstick, removes the lid, twists it up to observe the colour.*

EDITH: That *is* a great colour.

EDITH *looks down the front of her robe to fact check.*

Well there you go. Dior Stone Fruit.

ROSIE: While the serums settle in, I usually move to nails. Then base and face. Followed by hair. And lipstick last so you can go hard on prees. Or coffee in your case.

EDITH: Do we have time for nails?

ROSIE: We'll make time.

EDITH: It's not the priority.

ROSIE: If your hands are on the podium they'll likely be in frame.

EDITH: So?

ROSIE: So journos will see you've been biting them.

EDITH *folds her arms across her chest to hide her nails.*

I can file them back and do a neutral polish. Super simple. It'll only take a minute.

EDITH *nods to indicate she accepts.*

Nails take a few minutes. During the following, ROSIE *works quickly to clip and file off a few rough edges, then applies a coat of colour.*

EDITH: Is it easier to do your own makeup or someone else's?

ROSIE: Someone else for sure.

EDITH: Really?

ROSIE: One hundred percent.

EDITH: Well we're all our own worst critics.

ROSIE: What?

EDITH: We know our flaws so intimately.

ROSIE: When I do my own makeup, I have to use a mirror. And when you look in a mirror you're looking at a flat image.

EDITH: How do you mean?

ROSIE: Well a mirror is a flat surface, so what you're looking at is a flattened reflection. There's distortion. But in front of you, I don't see you that way. There's depth, there's shadows, there's constantly changing angles, and tiny shifts in your muscles. It's like I'm working with a sculpture. But when I do my own makeup, all I have is the reflection. So it's more like painting a canvas. And I might overcompensate. But that's not how people see me in real life.

EDITH: But that's the only way we ever see ourselves. Reflections. Or photographs. Or video. That's just …

Silence.

I find that really haunting.

Silence.

One of our think-tank projects looked at how often we catch glimpses of our reflection. In the past, it was two or three times a day. Morning and night at home in the mirror. Then over time, that crept up and up to eight times across the day. In the bathroom at work. But now? Well with socials and video calls, it's jumped to thirty-nine times. Observing ourselves. Either consciously or unconsciously.

ROSIE: You can quadruple that for me.

EDITH: Really?

ROSIE: Department store girl, so, *mirrors everywhere.*

Pause.

EDITH: Of course. Me too. Always surrounded by …

Pause.

Did you always see yourself becoming a makeup artist?

ROSIE *shrugs.*

Well, you have a gift.

ROSIE: I love it. I love helping women feel beautiful. I love that they walk out completely different to how they walk in. They just hold themselves different.

EDITH: Lots of things have that effect on people.

ROSIE: On women.

EDITH: Women are people.

> ROSIE *shrugs.*

ROSIE: When I was freelance, I'd get major clients, but really stressed about what to charge. Like, having to name my price and ask for money. In retail it's just easier. Plus I love my customers. The good ones tell me all their secrets and by the end of the hour we're besties.

EDITH: So you fell into it?

ROSIE: Well, I've always been really good at it. And my school life was shit. My attendance was pretty much a string of there, not there. And my parents, *well* … Were you close to your father?

EDITH: He was my best friend.

> *Beat.*

ROSIE: Big day for you.

EDITH: Yes.

ROSIE: Have you been picturing it in your head forever?

EDITH: Quite a bit recently.

ROSIE: You sound just like my brides.

EDITH: What?

ROSIE: Dreaming of this day.

EDITH: …

ROSIE: It's nice to have a moment of calm before the storm.

EDITH: …

ROSIE: Just us girls.

EDITH: …

ROSIE: Getting pampered before your big moment.

> *Rosie's phone rings. It's her new boyfriend, Johnny. She's set his ringtone to something obnoxious.*

Sorry! That's me. It'll be Johnny … My boyfriend … We only just started calling each other that … It's pretty new, but it's definitely a thing. It moved really fast because we just knew. So what's your husband like?

EDITH: Adam. Ambitious. He gets it. He's protective of me. Of our image.

ROSIE: How'd you meet?

EDITH: At a gala dinner my parents were hosting. I remember seeing him across the room, hand in his jacket pocket, slouching to hide his height. I forced an introduction and it made him nervous. The boss's daughter. But there was undeniable chemistry.

ROSIE: So you knew immediately?

EDITH: Right then and there.

ROSIE: Yeah, I knew about my boyfriend too.

EDITH: The public really rallied around us when Dad got sick. It's like unconsciously they knew. Like, we were next in line.

ROSIE: Johnny's a bit older. Like thirty. It's his birthday tonight actually. And he's nothing like the fuckwits my age. He's always spoiling me and taking me out and paying for dinner. He's really romantic like that. But he's also a feminist. Except for when it comes to paying for dinner. He's a co-owner at this gym franchise called Ropes Ropes Ropes. He got me working out with him which was a total game-changer. Completely cleared up my acne. You have no idea how rude people can be about your skin when you're a makeup artist.

EDITH: Okay you need to stop.

ROSIE: What?

EDITH: Talking.

ROSIE: Oh. I thought we were both—?

EDITH: I don't have time to do 'the chat' with you right now.

ROSIE: That's fine.

EDITH: I need to focus. Get myself in the right mindset.

Long pause.

ROSIE: [*checking nails*] Polish is dry so you're fine to …

She gestures 'move around'.

A knock on the door.

EDITH: Coffee!

EDITH *waits for* ROSIE.

ROSIE *waits for* EDITH.

Do you mind? I can't open the door looking like …

She gestures to herself.

ROSIE gets the door.

ROSIE returns with a pot of coffee and a stack of the morning's newspapers, which she dumps on the counter.

EDITH joins ROSIE and pours herself a coffee. She pops a couple of Panadol.

Black coffee and Panadol. Breakfast of champions.

ROSIE takes a second to flick through the magazine. She stops on Edith's 'What's in your handbag?' story.

So what do you think?

ROSIE: About what?

EDITH: About what's in my handbag.

ROSIE: …

EDITH: Say it.

ROSIE: *It's a bit …*

EDITH: It's bad.

ROSIE: Yeah, it's pretty bad.

EDITH: How bad though?

ROSIE: No left-field cult products, no personal touches, no virtue-signalling …

EDITH: So bad bad.

ROSIE: The headline's good.

EDITH: Fashion magazines are a minefield. It's impossible to frame what I say.

ROSIE: If you tell the truth it doesn't really matter what you say.

EDITH: I can't answer questions like 'what's in your handbag' truthfully.

ROSIE: Why? *What's in your handbag?*

EDITH: What would a bright, young woman such as yourself have wanted to see in my handbag?

ROSIE: Why don't you tell me what's actually in there and I'll tell you if it's any good.

EDITH: Nice try.

ROSIE: Come on. I think a modern icon would tell the truth about what's in her handbag.

EDITH accepts the challenge. She finds her handbag and begins rifling through it.

EDITH: Tic Tacs. Hand sanitiser. Lipstick. Blush. Blotting powder. Contact solution. Wallet. Second phone. Used makeup wipes. Empty packet of Panadol. Tampons. Boarding pass. Box of almonds. Two loose almonds from yesterday's box of almonds. And, like, a dozen loose business cards from dignitaries whose names I don't remember.

ROSIE: That's brilliant! You should have said those words exactly.

EDITH: There is no way my media team would have signed off on that.

ROSIE: People are obsessed with real details.

EDITH: What's in your handbag is a superficial premise.

ROSIE: But it's not superficial if you give an honest answer. If you're actually real about it, then you totally change the conversation.

> ROSIE's *body language indicates* EDITH *should sit down.* EDITH *doesn't take the hint.*

Shall we get started on glam?

> EDITH *takes a seat back in the makeup chair, taking one of the newspapers with her.*
>
> *Base takes a little longer than skin prep. During the following,* ROSIE *pumps foundation on her pallet, perhaps mixing a few to get the right shade, then applies it with a brush. Colour-corrects* EDITH's *under-eye circles. Spot conceals blemishes. Contours her cheekbones, nose and forehead.*

EDITH: [*reading a headline*] 'Daddy's dissociated princess takes the reins.' Ouch.

ROSIE: Is it strange seeing all that stuff in the papers?

EDITH: I grew up with my family in the papers. It'll be strange the day it stops.

> *Both women continue their work.*

I learned to read by staring at newspapers. Up on Dad's knee at the kitchen counter. He'd read out loud to me. It was my job to turn the pages. I'd get ink all over my fingers. See! [*Holding up her hands to show the ink on her fingertips*] Happens every morning.

ROSIE: Oh wow! I've got a wipe.

> ROSIE *gets a makeup wipe and cleans the ink off* EDITH's *fingertips. It's almost childlike.*

Sorry about your dad.

EDITH: Thank you.

ROSIE: He got sick or something?

EDITH: You didn't read about it?

ROSIE: I don't find politics very interesting.

> EDITH *bites her tongue, smiles at* ROSIE.

> ROSIE *smiles back.*

> EDITH *flicks to find a column and hands the newspaper to* ROSIE.

EDITH: Here.

> ROSIE *reluctantly puts down her makeup brushes.*

ROSIE: [*reading aloud*] 'A lifetime spent as a faithful family man, an upstanding Catholic, and a legendary Prime Minister. The family were grateful to have him pass away peacefully at home, surrounded by those who loved him.' That's nice.

EDITH: It is nice, isn't it. It's the Kennedys. It's the Roosevelts. There's a sense of romance about a family dynasty. There's my dad, there's me, and maybe one day Adam and I will make future little la-di-dahs to run the country.

ROSIE: Nepo babies are totally making a comeback.

EDITH: After he was diagnosed, it all moved very quickly. My father was such a dominant figure in the party, that there weren't any obvious alternative candidates. The Deputy was a moron. No, they needed an outsider. Fast-tracked. Tasha saw the opportunity. Adam crunched the numbers. And together they lined up the pieces.

> I buried my father on a Wednesday.
> Tasha was making deals that evening.
> We announced I'd be running in his seat five days later.
> By-election called.
> Campaigned well. Didn't put a foot wrong.
> Election last weekend.
> Landslide victory.
> Caucus endorsed me as their leader.
> Handed in my resignation at the Aldridge Institute.
> And here we are.
> In ninety minutes I'll be the youngest woman ever to run the country.

ROSIE: Wow.

EDITH: First day on the job. This morning, I give my inaugural address.

ROSIE: Did you know you were gonna win?

EDITH: I was very confident I could win leadership. I knew where the bodies were buried. I knew the kind of shit that went on. The kind of men he let rise. And I said to Tasha, alright, if I'm gonna do this, I wanna play aggressive. All the king's horses and all the king's men better brace themselves for a good-old-fashioned dinosaur cull.

ROSIE: I like this confidence.

EDITH: You have to be confident.

ROSIE: I can work with this confidence.

EDITH: You have to believe you're born to it. Then when the opportunity reveals itself …

ROSIE: Take it.

EDITH: Exactly.

ROSIE: I need to be more like that.

EDITH: No-one's going to hand it to you on a silver platter.

ROSIE: True that.

EDITH: There's something legitimate about snatching it. Snatching it makes it legitimate.

ROSIE: Well I am personally hyped for the looks you're gonna serve. Just swear to me you are not gonna start wearing florals.

EDITH: [*giving her a knowing look*] *Please.*

ROSIE: You know the lipstick you wore the night you won? NARS Dolce Vita.

EDITH: I thought you didn't find politics very interesting?

ROSIE: Not *politics* politics. But you? You're a celebrity. NARS Dolce Vita completely sold out at work this week. We tried to get stock moved from another store, but they sold out too. So we called our parent company. Same story. Had to place it on backorder from the distributor.

EDITH: Wow. That's …

ROSIE: You're a total influencer. Can I get a selfie with you later for my feed?

EDITH: Of course! Oh that reminds me. Comms keep demanding I post more 'getting ready' content. [*Passing* ROSIE *her phone*] Would you mind?

ROSIE: Please. I have mastered the dark arts of 'getting ready' content.

ROSIE *begins snapping away.* EDITH*'s a natural in front of the camera. She changes poses slightly with each frame. Perhaps she takes a sip of coffee from a campaign mug, stares out the window, ready to take on the day.*

Yes. You're a natural!

ROSIE *gives the phone back to* EDITH *who scrolls through the images.*

EDITH: I look old.

ROSIE: No you don't.

EDITH: I look tired. My skin's all—

ROSIE: Dry? I told you. Hydrate hydrate hydrate.

EDITH: I am a bit thirsty.

The hotel phone rings.

EDITH *nods to indicate* ROSIE *should answer it, while* EDITH *continues scrolling.*

ROSIE *does.*

ROSIE: [*on the phone*] Uh-huh? [*To* EDITH] {One-hour} call. [*On the phone*] Uh-huh. [*To* EDITH] Do we want breakfast?

EDITH *makes a face, 'No'.*

[*On the phone*] No breakfast. [*To* EDITH] Housekeeping says Adam pre-ordered.

EDITH: Tell the staff to eat it.

ROSIE: [*on the phone*] No breakfast, please. She hates the menu here.

ROSIE *hangs up.*

EDITH: I get tagged daily with a challenge to post a makeup-free selfie. 'No makeup. No filter, ladies. Go!' Actors, CEOs, media personalities all dutifully answer the call. The comments always say the same thing, 'You're stunning under there.' 'You look so much better without makeup.'

ROSIE: It takes a lot of work to look that understated.

EDITH: [*discovering a photo, showing it around to* ROSIE] This one's good.

ROSIE: [*glancing at the photo*] Love!

EDITH: I'll send it to Adam for approval.

ROSIE: Your husband?

EDITH: His team makes sure I look my best. Consider all possible interpretations of the caption. It's standard practice.

ROSIE: Johnny's like that too.

EDITH: Who?

ROSIE: *My boyfriend.*

EDITH: It helps to have a second pair of eyeballs.

ROSIE: Totally. He likes to see my pics before I post them.

EDITH: Well, I'm a public figure.

ROSIE: I used to post loads of mirror selfies and he said I looked a bit try-hard and he prefers it when I look more natural.

EDITH: That's not the same.

> *Edith's phone rings, she takes the call—slow and steady, she is an assassin.*

[*On the phone*] Mmm-hmm. An intimate part? An anus photo. Before breakfast?

> *A knock at the door.*

[*To* ROSIE] If it's breakfast, send it back.

> ROSIE *reluctantly puts down her makeup brushes to get the door.*

[*On the phone again*] I think it's important to remember that I'm not the one taking photos of my anus. [*Beat*] I don't want to condemn and move on.

ROSIE: [*to housekeeping, from offstage*] Stop it! She'll love them!

EDITH: [*on the phone*] No, listen. The shit my father turned a blind eye to: the intimidation, the harassment, the misuse of power, the back-door deals. It needs to end.

ROSIE: [*to* EDITH, *from offstage*] It's not breakfast!

EDITH: Well this isn't really my mess to clean up, mate. He's not the Deputy anymore.

> EDITH *hangs up.*

> ROSIE *enters carrying an enormous bouquet of flowers.*

ROSIE: They're gigantic!

> ROSIE *hands the bouquet to* EDITH.

> EDITH *rolls her eyes.*

EDITH: Couldn't've cost more than five hundred.

ROSIE: Five hundred on flowers?

EDITH: Could have gone bigger given the occasion.

ROSIE: No wonder they're gigantic.

EDITH: Well Adam can pay a gigantic price tag given he's not here this
    morning.

ROSIE: There's a card.

>   EDITH *gives the bouquet back to* ROSIE.

You're not even going to read the card?

EDITH: No.

ROSIE: Five hundred on flowers and she doesn't even read the card.

EDITH: Go on then.

>   ROSIE *unpins the card and reads it aloud.*

ROSIE: [*reading*] It says, 'Go get 'em, Edie! Celeste.'

>   EDITH*, shocked at first, snatches the card from* ROSIE *and reads
>   it for herself.*

Should I put them in water?

>   EDITH *takes the flowers off* ROSIE *and calmly walks across the
>   room. She pulls out a drawer that conceals a garbage bin and
>   drops the flowers and card inside.*

Not a fan of Celeste?

>   EDITH *returns to the chair, but turns back, and returns to the bin
>   to give the flowers the middle finger reasonably aggressively.*

Get it out of your system.

>   EDITH *returns to the makeup chair as if nothing happened.*

Women need to express their anger more. It's like scientifically a thing.
I'm working on it. Trying to feel a bit more in control. Trying to find
outlets that are a bit less 'cry-for-help' and a bit more 'self-honouring'.
I'm really starting to see some progress. I do loads of self-improvement.

EDITH: I don't.

ROSIE: Well, why would you? Nothing to improve on really.

EDITH: Women need to find hobbies beyond 'improving themselves'.
    Women who have time to improve themselves are bored. If they
    had something to do they wouldn't turn themselves into a project.

ROSIE: You do give me that vibe. That trash-compactor vibe.

EDITH: Excuse you?

ROSIE: One of those people who can just compact their trash deep down inside themselves. I aspire to be like that. Like you. It's heaps classier. Just to know how to compact your trash down and shut the fuck up. [*Gesturing to the bin*] So what was all that then?

EDITH: I've been sent hundreds of floral arrangements over the past months. Our home is drowning in native bouquets and sympathy wreaths and fruit hampers and fucking little native posies in fucking little mason jars. My dining room is bordering on an art installation.

ROSIE: Who's Celeste?

EDITH: Now might be one of those moments to shut the fuck up.

> *Pause.*

Sorry. This isn't the succession I imagined.

ROSIE: … You're grieving. It's fine.

EDITH: His last words to me were—

> *She stops herself.*

Something stupid about Monopoly.

ROSIE: The board game?

EDITH: We played that final night together. A family tradition.

ROSIE: So wholesome.

EDITH: More of a blood sport for us.

ROSIE: So who won?

EDITH: … I did.

ROSIE: He let you win.

EDITH: No. I won properly.

ROSIE: It's like he knew he was handing it all to you.

EDITH: No. He was far too flashy to win. Had fun splashing cash. Park Lane and Mayfair. Always did terrible trades for Trafalgar Square because it's where he met Mum.

ROSIE: I'd always be the shoe.

EDITH: [*correcting*] The boot.

ROSIE: And go for yellows.

EDITH: Wrong.

ROSIE: What?

EDITH: You go for yellows you lose.

ROSIE: I mean, that's not a thing. Is it?

EDITH: 'Going for yellows' is terrible strategy.

ROSIE: I'm pretty sure I won at least a few times.

EDITH: Depends who your opponents were, I suppose.

ROSIE: It's a game of chance.

EDITH: Is it?

ROSIE: You roll a dice.

EDITH: Choices matter far more than any roll of a dice.

ROSIE: …

EDITH: I'm pretty competitive. Runs in the family.

ROSIE: Wait, *actually* yellows you lose?

EDITH: Yes.

ROSIE: How do you know?

EDITH: Because I always win.

ROSIE: Why?

EDITH: Because I'm very good at Monopoly.

ROSIE: What colours do you go for?

EDITH: Whatever I land on.

ROSIE: That's chance.

EDITH: You want to buy every single property you land on, even if you have to mortgage other properties to get the cash. Buying up as much property as possible gives you the best chance to control the board early. Plus, you need properties to make trades. Yellows are fine, but oranges are the best.

ROSIE: I thought you buy whatever you land on?

EDITH: Oranges are landed on more than any other property for several reasons. One, the most landed-on square is Jail because there are so many ways to get there. Jail puts you one roll away from the oranges. The 'Advance to Pall Mall' card puts you one roll away from the oranges. 'Go Back Three Spaces' puts you on Vine Street; an orange. 'Advance to the Nearest Utility' puts you on Electric Company two out of three times, which is, that's right …

ROSIE: One roll away from the oranges?

EDITH: Go for orange if you can.

ROSIE: Thanks for the tip.

EDITH: AND buy as many houses as you can as quickly as you can. There are only thirty-two houses available. Once those houses are gone, no-one else can build. You can soak up twenty of the thirty-two houses on the cheapest strip of property alone.

ROSIE: Wow, that's …

EDITH: Strategy.

ROSIE: Soak up all the houses, huh?

EDITH: Yep.

ROSIE: But then there's no houses for anyone else. You know, if that's what they were planning to do with their turn.

EDITH: They're your opponents.

ROSIE: Kinda sucks the fun out of it.

EDITH: Winning is fun.

ROSIE: Fun is fun.

EDITH: I have fun when I win.

Edith's phone rings.

[*On the phone*] Tasha! Thank goodness.

Is that a joke?

That's not good enough.

No, listen! Two of our donors are on the board of Qantas!

Well would they *fly through fog* for a male PM, because I think they would!

Right. Your ETA?

Uh-huh. Uh-huh … Uh-huh.

EDITH *quietly hangs up the phone.*

EDITH *sits in silence.*

Perhaps EDITH *smashes her coffee cup in the sink or screams into a pillow.*

This is a bad omen.

ROSIE: It's totally not a bad omen.

EDITH: The history books are going to trace everything back to this exact moment as the moment where everything began to unravel.

ROSIE: So the fog hasn't cleared?

EDITH: This fucking fog is my downfall. Comms, Chief of Staff, EA, PA, campaign chair, my husband! All stuck in Melbourne! No. No way. I am not going out there without my team.

ROSIE: I need to start colour-correcting.

EDITH: I need to think.

ROSIE: Probably best if you think at the same time I do your makeup.

EDITH: Put the {primer} down, Rosie.

ROSIE: I need to get started.

EDITH: I mean it!

ROSIE: I only have ninety minutes with you.

EDITH: My dark circles are not the priority right now.

ROSIE: If I have to rush today, you'll look as chaotic on the outside as you're feeling on the inside and everyone will be able to see.

EDITH: I'm gonna throw up.

ROSIE: You're getting clammy again.

EDITH: Because I'm going to throw up!

ROSIE: Edith, stop! Look at me. I'm about to say something important.

> EDITH *looks at her.*

I'm pretty shit at most things. I'm a terrible friend. I've cheated on boyfriends. I have a scary addiction to Afterpay and no impulse control. I don't know the date of my own mother's birthday. BUT! I am very *very* good at makeup. And I promise that with my powers, you are going to look and feel like a dope ass qween when you walk out that door. And all you need to do is sit in this chair while I get to work. And then you can throw one of those designer frocks on your slammin' bod and you're good to go. You're gonna walk out that door and absolutely slay today.

EDITH: Okay.

ROSIE: You can do this.

EDITH: Everything has to meet expectations.

ROSIE: I won't let you down. [*Beat*] Now. This is *very* important. Will you be in natural or studio light today?

EDITH: The photographs will be on the lawns outside.

ROSIE: Natural light. Let's swatch by the window.

> ROSIE *manoeuvres* EDITH *to the window. She opens the curtains so she can examine* EDITH*'s skintone in the morning light.*

Huh! You're cool-toned in natural light. No wonder you have so many freckles. We should let people see them.

EDITH: I don't think so.

ROSIE: Super fresh face. Light to medium coverage, killer brows, lippy, we'll accent the eyes. It's a crazy amount of effort to pull off truly flawless no-makeup makeup, but I think you can pull it off.

EDITH: No-makeup makeup doesn't fucking mean anything.

ROSIE: It flaunts a more down-to-earth, nothing-to-hide attitude. To nail it, you need to embrace showing off some imperfections.

EDITH: Problematic word choice.

ROSIE: Freckles, beauty spots, some pigmentation. You'll look equal parts fresh and flawless without appearing to have made any effort at all.

EDITH: No, no, we're not doing that.

ROSIE: Doing what?

EDITH: Going off script. Do your job and cover it all up.

ROSIE: Girl, you do not need to cover up.

EDITH: [*referring to the magazine*] This is the look I need to maintain.

ROSIE: Sure. And what look is that?

EDITH: … Aspirational.

ROSIE: And what about this look is aspirational to you exactly?

EDITH: It's just a vibe.

ROSIE: Uh-huh. And aren't I the sort of person who should find you aspirational?

EDITH: You said I look hot.

ROSIE: Oh, you're slaying. No-one's debating you're a ten outta ten. But it's so quintessentially manicured that it tells me nothing about you. Like, what's the colour story? What are you wearing today?

EDITH: A dress.

ROSIE: What does it look like?

EDITH: [*doing a terrible job at explaining*] Well it sort of goes out like … and then has these really intricate … and sort of tight around the … and big statement in the … [*Giving up*] It's on the rack.

ROSIE *makes her way to the garment bags. She surveys the various outfits.*

ROSIE: Which one is it?

EDITH: They're all labelled on the hangers.

ROSIE *flicks through the dresses.*

ROSIE: What are all these for?

EDITH: Contingency dresses. In case the weather changes, something spills, a state funeral happens at the last minute, a wall I'm standing in front of turns out to be the same colour as my outfit. That happened last week actually.

ROSIE: No pantsuits?

EDITH: [*giving her a knowing look*] Please.

> ROSIE *unzips the garment bag containing the Chanel dress.*

ROSIE: [*riffing on 'the future is bright'*] The fuchsia is bright.

EDITH: The fuchsia is very bright.

ROSIE: With this dress, let's do a bright-red lip.

EDITH: Red will be too loud.

ROSIE: You may as well use it to say something.

EDITH: And what does red say?

ROSIE: It says you don't fuck around.

> EDITH *smiles.*

EDITH: We decided a pink dress was too obvious. I'm wearing the navy.

ROSIE: But it's perfect.

EDITH: It's not my look.

ROSIE: [*gesturing to the pink dress*] Whatever *this is*, should be your look.

EDITH: [*dismissive*] Please. I'm a seasoned political operator, Rosie. I founded a social research think tank on emerging public trends. I think I know a thing or two about what dress to wear.

ROSIE: Word salad. All I'm hearing is word salad.

EDITH: There is a *strategy*.

ROSIE: With this dress, you don't need a strategy.

EDITH: The overwhelming advice is to get a uniform and stick to it.

ROSIE: A uniform.

EDITH: That way people will listen rather than look.

ROSIE: And never express yourself?

EDITH: I express myself through rigorous discourse. Not fashion.

ROSIE: Okay. [*Finding an alternative*] In that case … [*Pulling one out*] You should go for orange.

EDITH: What's wrong with the navy?

ROSIE: [*holding up the navy dress*] *This* gives me *nothing*.

EDITH: That dress was decided on by a team of experts who took into consideration the demographics of my supporters, the tone of the occasion, the economics of local design, the fabric, the cut, the global footprint of the garment, the cost per wear. Everything.

> ROSIE *looks at the navy again, she pulls a face.*

A whole team of stylists put together my outfit for today.

ROSIE: Fine. It's not like it's your wedding day.

EDITH: Wait, what does that mean?

ROSIE: It's not like everything's riding on this one dress.

EDITH: Everything *is* riding on this one dress! These photographs are going to be all over the world tomorrow. They'll be in newspapers, yes, but also in history books. In museums. If I have a heroic life— and I plan to—they'll create a monument to me. And when they commission the artist, they'll be given reference images. They won't be images of me old and shrunken over. Images of the woman who actually did the heroic things. They'll make it in the image of how I am now. Perhaps how I look today. Perhaps in this dress. Perhaps it will sit in the gardens here. And little girls will visit me on school excursions.

ROSIE: Well with that in mind, what do *you* want to wear?

EDITH: That's completely irrelevant.

ROSIE: Because I think, deep down, you kinda wanna wear the orange.

EDITH: I can't change a decision without consulting my team.

ROSIE: Well, it's just you and me in the room.

EDITH: No, you're wrong. Let's settle this.

> EDITH *takes the orange dress from* ROSIE, *drops her robe and changes outfit.*
>
> ROSIE, *without missing a beat, grabs Edith's robe and helps zip up the dress.*
>
> EDITH *smooths out the dress, takes a look in the mirror, and is taken aback.*

Oh my God, you're right!

ROSIE: You look FIRE!

EDITH: Alright. So we'll do the orange dress. And no-makeup makeup, like you said. What would you suggest for hair with this neckline?

ROSIE: [*moving her fingers through the length*] Hmm … Your hair's in much better condition than your skin.

EDITH: Three hundred dollars for a trim every eight weeks.

ROSIE: Hair is the most logical piece of the puzzle. If you're wearing designer clothes with minimalist makeup your hair needs to be the perfect transition between the two.

EDITH: Which is?

ROSIE: High-class. Low-key.

EDITH: I like that.

ROSIE: Relaxed, effortless waves, swept up into a pony. Keep it youthful with nods to Parisian, low-fuss romance. Perhaps some soft waves at the front.

EDITH: I don't want to look too …

ROSIE: Too what?

EDITH: Too girly.

ROSIE: You are a girl.

EDITH: Don't need to signpost it.

ROSIE: But you are a girl.

EDITH: Nothing too fussy. My usual person keeps it natural.

ROSIE: Soft waves will look natural. Natural natural will just be frizz. We don't want frizz.

EDITH: Soft waves it is.

ROSIE: Yes yes yes yes yes yes yes. It's coming together!

EDITH: Unzip me.

> EDITH *turns around.* ROSIE *unzips the dress, but her bracelet gets caught.*

Ouch you've / caught my—

ROSIE: Hang on it's my bracelet, it's stuck—

EDITH: What are / you—?!

ROSIE: SORRY! It's always getting caught on things!

EDITH: Stop pulling—!

ROSIE: Shit, it's the crucifix charm.

EDITH: Pinch the clasp.

ROSIE: If I pull, it's going to rip—

EDITH: I said *pinch*—

ROSIE: It's going to rip if I pull it—

EDITH: DON'T RIP IT!

ROSIE: I'M NOT GOING TO I said IF I pull / which I'm not—

EDITH: Let go let go / let go let go let go let go!

ROSIE: I've almost got it!

> ROSIE *gets it untangled.*

There! It's done!

EDITH *slips out of the orange dress and back into her robe. Fuming but holding it together.*

EDITH: [*tying her robe*] *That thing* is a work health and safety hazard.
ROSIE: I know, it's so gauche.

EDITH *takes a seat back in the makeup chair.*

EDITH: Perhaps not work appropriate given the risk to the garments.
ROSIE: Oh, I never take it off. All my girls from school have one.

ROSIE *moves on to* EDITH*'s face, making careful work to accent her eyes. During the following, she applies eyeshadow, eyeliner, mascara, and brows. She finishes with a few sweeps of highlighter to complete the look.*

We went to a Catholic girls' college, so it was like no jewellery, no piercings, no nail polish, no makeup, no hair dye, no self-expression basically. BUT we were allowed to wear the crucifix. So for birthdays we'd go hunting for the chunkiest, sparkliest, most bedazzled crucifixes we could find, so we could wear friendship bracelets and get away with it. It's completely tacky and horrible, but I love it. They're pretty much my soulmates. We had a bit of a fight the other day, actually.

EDITH: [*looking in the mirror*] You're right, hair back, natural waves, swept up into a pony.
ROSIE: I cancelled dinner last minute to pick up an extra shift. And now they're like 'withholding' forgiveness.
EDITH: Oh just ignore that crap. The amount of engagement parties and baby showers and milestone birthdays I haven't shown up to. Not by choice. Part of the job description. But the people you're meant to take through life always come around.
ROSIE: Really?
EDITH: So far.
ROSIE: They don't hold it against you?
EDITH: Some do, but less so if you're honest about what you want.

ROSIE *smiles. She hangs the orange dress back up on a hanger and delicately smooths out any wrinkles.*

ROSIE: I used to think not in a million parallel universes would I want to swap lives with someone like you. But waking up in hotels like this, and getting sent all these free clothes, is definitely opening my eyes to the possibility.

EDITH: Well they're not 'free clothes'.

ROSIE: Shit, who pays for all this?

EDITH: The taxpayer.

ROSIE: What?

EDITH: My non-essentials budget.

>   *Beat.*

ROSIE: Wait. My taxes pay for your clothes?

EDITH: My taxes pay for your mum's disability pension.

ROSIE: … How do you know that about my mum?

EDITH: We background checked you before we reached out.

ROSIE: Oh.

>   *Pause.*

I guess that makes sense.

>   *Pause.*

So then you'd know about … ? My savings situation? I guess it's not technically savings. It's actually the opposite of savings. Like, 'debt', I guess you would call it.

EDITH: Nothing came up.

ROSIE: Well that makes sense. Afterpay isn't technically debt. But yeah it does feel a bit … Actually literally even thinking about that app makes my heart go a bit palpitate-y.

EDITH: Oh yeah, those 'buy now pay later' apps are all the rage.

ROSIE: They're pretty addictive.

EDITH: The alcopops of the finance world.

ROSIE: Alcopops?

EDITH: Cruisers. Double Blacks. Ruskis.

ROSIE: What do you mean?

EDITH: Same alcohol content and nothing but sugar water.

ROSIE: I like Cruisers.

EDITH: I get that young people like them. But as a product? A pre-mix is cheap.

ROSIE: They're actually pretty expensive.

EDITH: I mean *cheap*. Void of any refinement, any elevation. No agricultural history, no craftsmanship from people who know what to do with the raw materials.

ROSIE: God, you're a bourgie bitch.

EDITH: It's the same with those apps. If you're going to use credit, *really use it*. You know?

ROSIE: No.

EDITH: It's the boot theory.

ROSIE: Never heard of it.

EDITH: Let's say a great pair of leather boots—RM Williams for example—cost seven hundred dollars? But an affordable pair of boots, maybe made of PCV, which are sort of okay for a season or two before they fall apart, cost seventy dollars.

ROSIE: Yeah?

EDITH: Well a great pair of boots, that are well made, can last for years. So someone who can afford RM Williams has a pair of shoes that will still be keeping their feet dry in ten years. While a less well-off person may end up spending hundreds of dollars anyway, wearing through shitty-quality shoes, season after season, and by the time ten years have passed, still have nothing.

ROSIE: Yeah, but who wants to wear the same pair of shoes for ten years?

EDITH: My point is, *that's* how you should be using credit. To level the playing field. Not to flit away your paycheck on eyeshadow palettes and setting spray.

ROSIE: You know I'm a makeup artist right? I buy makeup.

EDITH: Mmm.

ROSIE: Seriously. Do you think I'd even be in this room if Tasha hadn't stalked my social feed after the fundraiser? Accounts don't look that lit without some dollars invested in my looks.

EDITH: Okay, sure, but for the general population, makeup is—

ROSIE: Part of the non-essentials budget?

EDITH: Right.

ROSIE: Pretty essential today.

EDITH: You're smart. Just … be smart about credit.

ROSIE: What, so I can buy one of those thirty-two houses the boomers already soaked up?

EDITH: …

ROSIE: It's not technically credit anyway. People my age don't 'do' credit cards. I don't think I've ever stepped foot inside a literal bank.

EDITH: If someone else is fronting the bill, it's credit.

ROSIE: Well it can't be credit because I didn't do a credit check. You don't need one. All you need is a bank account and mobile number, and you're instantly approved. Then every purchase gets split into four payments, so it's more affordable. *And* it's interest-free. Technically. I mean there are late fees.

EDITH: How much are late fees?

ROSIE: Like ten bucks. Plus seven bucks for every week you don't pay.

EDITH: So you could pay more in late fees than you did for the item?

ROSIE: It caps out at sixty-eight dollars … but yeah. It's a grey area.

EDITH: How much do you owe exactly?

ROSIE: I dunno. I use a couple of different ones. Afterpay, Zip, Latitude, Brighte, plus a few others. So it's kinda split up into all these repayments across like six different apps … so the numbers get a bit … jumbled.

EDITH: What's the time?

ROSIE: {Six twenty-six.}

EDITH: I should practise my speech. Can you pass my papers?

> ROSIE *begrudgingly passes* EDITH *her folders.*

> *After a moment.*

I need a pen.

> ROSIE *picks up a pen that* EDITH *could probably reach herself and holds it out to* EDITH. *Before* EDITH *can take it,* ROSIE *snatches it out of reach.*

ROSIE: Have you noticed how you do that?

EDITH: Do what?

ROSIE: Get me to fetch and carry for you?

EDITH: Oh, *that*?

ROSIE: I'm here to do your makeup.

EDITH: No no no, that's not what that was.

ROSIE: Wasn't it?

EDITH: Normally there's like ten people in this room, so it would be like one thing per person.

ROSIE: Uh-huh.

EDITH: I'm under quite a lot of pressure this morning.

ROSIE: Oh sorry, do you want to look like shit?

EDITH: It's a pen. It took you five seconds.

ROSIE: I think this would be much nicer for both of us, if you just pretend we're equal.

> EDITH *eyes* ROSIE, *considers arguing with this.* ROSIE *holds* EDITH*'s gaze, maybe even smiles.*
>
> EDITH *decides against it.*
>
> EDITH *flicks through her papers to find her speech. Then sits up straight, composes herself and closes her eyes.*
>
> EDITH *goes through her speech moment by moment in her head.*

You can say it out loud if you need to.

EDITH: Visualisation technique, it's what all the elite athletes do.

ROSIE: Helps with the nerves.

EDITH: I'm not nervous.

ROSIE: My brides always practise their vows out loud before the big moment.

EDITH: You need to stop talking so I can focus.

> EDITH *keeps moving slightly as she imagines her big moment. This makes* ROSIE *a bit uncomfortable, but she continues to work.*

ROSIE: …

EDITH: …

ROSIE: …

EDITH: …

ROSIE: …

EDITH: …

ROSIE: …

EDITH: Is everything okay between us?

ROSIE: You told me to stop talking.

EDITH: …

ROSIE: …

EDITH: …

ROSIE: …

EDITH: Normally there's a lot of noise around.

ROSIE: …

EDITH: Chatter.

ROSIE: …

EDITH: White noise.

ROSIE: …

EDITH: Ambience.

ROSIE: …

EDITH: It helps me not get distracted.

ROSIE: …

EDITH: Maybe some white noise would be beneficial.

ROSIE: You want me to keep talking, but not talk directly to you?

EDITH: Would you mind?

ROSIE: What should I talk about?

EDITH: Whatever you like.

ROSIE: Okay, sure. No pressure. Just some gentle, ambient chit-chat for the PM. Ah … I like your robe. It's nice. Nice thread count, feels like. The last thing I bought online was a robe.

On Afterpay. Of course. Last week. Who even knows what I bought the week before that. Probably my gel nails, and whatever was in my last MECCA haul, and coffee before work and lunch at work and drinks after work and like a dress if we went out and whatever activewear was on sale last month.

I got a bit behind on repayments and Johnny started to suspect. And I didn't want him to freak out, so I told him it was like 2K. And he freaked out. But then was so seriously nice about it and paid it off for me so the late fees wouldn't keep piling up.

But it was way way more than 2K. And I absolutely cannot tell him.

He's great, but you know how some people can be funny about things they don't understand?

I think I'm really starting to get a handle on it though. I figured out what sets me off. Like last week Johnny and I had this huge blow-up and normally I'd get all worked up and go on a spending rage. And I nearly did. I got out of the car and I marched straight through the food court to David Jones. Ground floor Accessories. And just started grabbing whatever I wanted off the displays. Sequin clutch, sunglasses, silk scarves, earrings, bangles, bucket hat. Across to

Intimates. Silk slip, shapewear, lace bras, regular bras, bodysuit, swimsuit, bikini top. Take the escalator two flights up to House and Home. Egyptian cotton sheets, stemless wine glasses, bath robe, bath salts, vision board, fragrance diffuser. And I get to the register. And Berny—middle-aged man with bleached hair—starts ringing it up. And he's scanning it all, and the register is climbing climbing climbing and the beeps start sounding hypnotic. Lipstick, lip gloss, eyeshadow quad, setting spray. And Berny says 'Twenty-seven hundred' and I say, 'No problem' and he says, 'Cash or card?' and I say 'Buy Now Pay Later, Berny.' And I get out my phone, and I open the app. And I make the purchase. And then I ask myself, 'Did that choice honour me?' And I smile at Berny and say, 'I'm gonna need to make a return.' And IT'S A RUSH. Knowing how to short-circuit myself. Knowing how to disrupt my own bullshit. Just binge return binge return binge return binge return to blow off steam. So now when Johnny and I have blow-ups, I know how to express my anger in a healthy way.

EDITH: ... You have 'blow-ups' often?

ROSIE: How often do you and Adam fight?

EDITH: Never.

ROSIE: Yeah yeah, perfect life, perfect marriage.

EDITH: It's definitely not perfect.

    Beat.

Maybe it would be good to say it out loud. If that's alright?

ROSIE: So long as I can keep {blending}.

    EDITH *goes to speak then stops. She's nervous.*

EDITH: I've been picturing this moment. My first words in the role. Alright, so, I'll go up to the podium ... and I'll take a breath ... and then, 'We all carry the voice of our father. Deep within. We carry their blood. So even before we become ourselves, their voice whispers to us. At the root of who we are is our father's voice. We resist what this might illuminate about our thoughts, our actions, our households, our society, our laws, and our great country. Even though I stand alone in this, I know I'm not, because his voice still guides me. I promise you that.'

EDITH *looks to* ROSIE, ROSIE *gives her nothing.*

Powerful, right?

ROSIE: …

EDITH: What?

ROSIE: You don't think it's a bit—?

EDITH *searches* ROSIE*'s face,* ROSIE *gives her nothing. Then,*

[*Overcompensating*] I'm sure you're gonna kill it.

EDITH: You hate it?

ROSIE: Anyone ever told you, you talk about your dad a lot?

EDITH: It's symbolic.

ROSIE *gives her a look, 'Really?'*

We're out of context. When you've done your thing and I'm wearing the dress and I'm up there … It'll all come together.

ROSIE: Really screams 'daddy issues'.

EDITH: I have to say *something* about him.

ROSIE: Well definitely don't say that.

EDITH: All of the advice has been to pay tribute.

ROSIE: Then give them something personal.

EDITH: It's a big mess at the moment.

ROSIE: Even better. It's real.

EDITH: No, I'm not … *that.*

ROSIE: Real?

EDITH: Listen, I know what you're trying to get at. But my version of *that*, my version of *authentic*, isn't cute. It's not quirky and endearing like you are. I'm … *a lot.* I'm emotional. And too much. It's completely unlikeable.

ROSIE: Well you got like a million votes, so clearly people like you.

EDITH: Sixty-two percent of the popular vote. Women came out in droves to vote for me.

ROSIE: [*encouraging*] Uh-huh.

EDITH: Forty-five percentage points more than my opponent. Though two points less than my father.

ROSIE: See! People like you. So give them more of you.

EDITH *glances at her speech.*

EDITH: I guess it does read a bit, *you know.*

ROSIE: *Right?* And you're Edith Aldridge. A modern icon.

EDITH: Newspapers keep calling me 'modern' as if it's the ultimate praise. 'She's so modern.' 'Such a modern woman.' It's code for young, beautiful, ambitious. She must adore literature, good wine, high-street fashion, charity balls, blowjobs, foreign policy, foreign cinema. I stand up for reproductive rights while maintaining respect among the conservatives, because as a modern woman I'm extremely fucking likeable to both sides. I'm well-dressed, well-spoken and well-behaved. I'm open-minded. I kept my surname. I don't get whiney or judgey or freak out when I'm in the wrong. You can trash-talk me, call me out, cancel me. I probably deserve it. I'll take a look at myself. I'll apologise. Because I'm a modern woman. But guess what? 'Modern women', like 'no-makeup makeup', doesn't fucking mean what it means.

ROSIE: Because you're not giving them human stuff.

EDITH: I'd rather not disclose the human stuff.

ROSIE: People love human stuff.

EDITH: I'm not one of those snowflakes who can just go out there with no makeup and no script and wing it.

ROSIE: Whoa, whoa, whoa. No-one's saying wing it. Don't go out there *with no makeup. With no script.* I'm just saying don't go out there *with that look, saying those words.* You know? No-makeup makeup, babe. Split the diff.

EDITH *returns to her speech.*

Listen, when I started at David Jones, customers saw right through me any time I said 'flawless complexion', 'forty-eight-hour staying power', 'liquid Botox'. And I never made sales targets. But then I dropped the script, and started being honest and saying, 'I got straight-up tequila drunk at the work Christmas party while I was wearing this eyeliner. I sweated my tits off on the dance floor. I cried in the bathrooms. I puked in the Uber. I woke up with smudged lipstick down my face, body bronzer on my clothes, Dorito crumbs in my hair. BUT I still had PERFECT eyeliner.' I've never made more sales.

Beat.

EDITH: Why don't you stay on tonight? I need hair and makeup for the formal functions. And touch-ups throughout the evening.

ROSIE: For real?

EDITH: Full face, different outfit, your call on hair.

ROSIE: Oh, wow, that's, yeah, I totally would, but—

EDITH: Are you in or out?

ROSIE: It's Johnny's birthday.

EDITH: So?

ROSIE: We have plans. I'm meeting his friends for the first time.

EDITH: You can't meet them some other night?

ROSIE: It's like a whole thing.

> *Rosie's phone rings. It's Johnny's ringtone. She blocks the call.*

EDITH: I'll double your fee.

ROSIE: Errr—

EDITH: You need to put yourself first more. I can tell.

ROSIE: By putting you first?

EDITH: Exactly. In this situation, putting me first is putting you first.

ROSIE: *I really want to.*

EDITH: Great. I'll book you for the full day. Tasha will sort it out with you later.

ROSIE: It's just this party's kind of a big deal. I haven't met these people before and I already splurged on this killer jumpsuit and dinner's like ninety bucks a head and he already paid for me, even though it's his birthday so technically I should be the one to—

EDITH: Oh God, I used to be like you.

ROSIE: Like what?

EDITH: Thinking everyone's approval mattered.

ROSIE: You still do.

EDITH: Yes, but now it *actually* matters. I literally have an approval rating.

ROSIE: Can I think about it?

> *Pause.*

EDITH: You need to learn how to prioritise. You need to decide what you're willing to be hated over and what you hope to be loved for. That's power.

> *Johnny calls again.*

ROSIE: Oh my God, he's gonna keep calling till I answer.

EDITH: So tell him now.

ROSIE: Tell him what?

EDITH: That you got a better offer.

ROSIE: I'm not saying that.

EDITH: It's the truth.

ROSIE: *Yeah, but.*

EDITH: Then lie! Make something up. Or say you're going and then
don't go.

> *A suspended pause as the obnoxious ringtone fills the space
> between them.* ROSIE *concedes.*

ROSIE: Just quickly then.

> ROSIE *takes the call. When she talks to Johnny, her voice changes
> into a baby voice which makes* EDITH *extremely uncomfortable.*

[*On the phone, full baby voice*] Hi baby, on your way to Ropes
Ropes Ropes? Yeah I got here okay, it was really cold though …
I know, I forgot my puffer … Yeah, I found my way okay. It was a
bit confusing, but the people at the front desk were so nice … About
tonight, Ms Aldridge just asked if I wanted to work late? … *Yeah
obviously!* … No, I wanted *you* to know that I said no already …
Okay I gotta go, I'm working … On three … You count … I like it
when you count … Byeeeeeee.

> ROSIE *hangs up.*

> *Beat.*

What?

EDITH: Here I was thinking you were Little Miss Authentic.

ROSIE: [*under her breath*] Ugh, whatever.

EDITH: I could take lessons from you.

ROSIE: It's the hours working in retail.

EDITH: You're a natural.

ROSIE: Just slap on that retail smile.

EDITH: [*laughing*] His face when you stand him up tonight.

ROSIE: Yeah, I think I'm gonna go.

EDITH: *Why?*

ROSIE: Because he's my boyfriend.

EDITH: You can't even be honest with him.

ROSIE: He was seriously so nice when I told him about my shopping stuff.

EDITH: So now you, what? *Owe him?*

ROSIE: Kind of.

EDITH: What, forever?

ROSIE: No, not forever.

EDITH: So how long?

ROSIE: I don't know.

EDITH: Till you pay him back?

ROSIE: I don't think it's a 'I have to pay him back' kind of thing.

EDITH: But you are though. In some way.

ROSIE: Sure. Maybe.

EDITH: So when will you be even?

ROSIE: It doesn't work like that exactly.

EDITH: If this is a great opportunity, and you're turning it down, out of what? Obligation? I'm just wondering how long you plan on doing that?

ROSIE: *He really helped me out.*

EDITH: And he'll always want something for that.

ROSIE: You've literally never met him.

EDITH: More loyalty, more sacrifice, more proof.

ROSIE: Okay, unsolicited.

EDITH: I don't understand why someone as smart as you would look me in the eye and say, 'Can I think about it?'

ROSIE: … I need to start on hair and get you downstairs in {half an hour}.

> *During the following,* ROSIE *styles Edith's hair. She gently combs it out, spritzes it with heat protector and sections it off to add a few waves to the front with a hair straightener. She teases the top section, then styles it back into a pony. At moments,* ROSIE *passes the hair straightener to* EDITH *to hold when she needs two hands.*

> *Silence at first as* ROSIE *sets up. Then, breaking the silence—*

So last night I was trying to figure out my look for dinner. And I did a practice run for hair and makeup. And Johnny got home. And I was wearing the jumpsuit. And he made a comment about how good I looked. And he asked, 'What's that for?' And it was meant to be a surprise so I said, 'It's not for anything, babe, mind your own business.' But then he got real quiet and I could tell he was mad.

He says, 'Looks expensive. You promised me you'd run that sorta stuff by me from now on. You know, as a buffer.'

So I tell him it's for his birthday. For meeting his friends.

And he was like, 'They're adults, babe. It's a bit much for them.'

And I say, 'Well, this is what I'm wearing.'

And he says, 'So don't come then if you're gonna be this difficult.'

EDITH: I feel like that too sometimes.

ROSIE: Like what?

EDITH: Like I'm pretending everything's fine when it isn't.

> EDITH *squeezes* ROSIE's *arm. It's the first contact they've had like this the whole play.*

> EDITH *returns to her speech again.*

ROSIE: Chin up.

EDITH: It's impossible to—

ROSIE: Hold there.

EDITH: Ouch.

ROSIE: Perfect.

EDITH: You're right. It's terrible.

ROSIE: Your speech?

EDITH: I need to be honest, like you said.

ROSIE: So rewrite it.

> EDITH *hesitates.*

I'll get you a pen.

> ROSIE *picks up Edith's pen and hands it to her.*

We need to feel really inspired.

EDITH: Right: be aspirational.

ROSIE: Not too aspirational though, because it still has to be relatable.

EDITH: Mmm. Create a mirror in which they might recognise themselves.

ROSIE: A flattering mirror.

EDITH: Right.

ROSIE: You got this.

EDITH: And this speech is in public so actual people need to actually hear it and actually feel something. The words need to get under their skin and *do something* to them.

ROSIE: Well it's just you and me in the room right now. If I asked you about your strength, where it all started, so I can be strong like you, you would say?

EDITH: You learn to be strong. You learn to have grit. Enthusiasm is common, but endurance is rare. I can still hear his voice, '*We're not raising some prissy private-school girl.*' I wasn't wrapped in cotton wool. Ever.

So finding that strength … Oh, this one moment jumps out. At school we had swimming days. Everyone had to tread water with clothes on. It's what we were working up to. The day came and I felt clammy just thinking about it. When I got to school the teacher said, 'Edith, you look like a ghost!' and said I better sit it out.

When I got home Mum and Dad asked, 'Well, how'd you do?' And I said, 'Top in class. I moved up a group!' And I pulled everything out of my school bag, and of course my swimming clothes came out, and they weren't wet. So they knew I'd lied.

Then Dad grabbed me by the wrist, and marched me outside, and without any warning THREW me in the pool. I sank. I tried to move my arms and my legs but my blazer and stockings were heavy. I felt my toes skim the bottom, so I knew if I could push up I could get to the top. So I pushed as hard as I could, and my face lifted above the surface, and I tried to tread water. But my face kept dipping under. And then Dad reached in. And pulled me out. And said, '*If you're afraid of something, you just do it! That's the only way to get on with your life!*'

Silence.

ROSIE: You really hated him.

EDITH: What?

ROSIE: I said you must have really hated him.

EDITH: … I didn't say that.

Pause.

I idolised him.

ROSIE *says nothing.*

He taught me how to be strong, how to handle all this.

ROSIE: You were terrified of him.

EDITH: No, no, I had a father like him so, so, I could become a person like me.

ROSIE: And that's the picture you want to give little girls?

EDITH *is knocked.*

EDITH: I just, um—

I don't know if I can have this conversation.

She looks like she might faint.

ROSIE: Don't worry! We're gonna armour you up! You'll look fierce, you'll feel fierce. I'm calling this look, 'Fierce. Funeral. Vibes.'

EDITH: I can't look like I'm going to my funeral.

ROSIE: You're gonna look powerful. Like the mistress at a funeral. Beside the woman whose scumbag husband finally carked it. She's been laying low in the shadows, but now it's her time to shine.

EDITH: Celeste certainly looked the part at Dad's funeral.

ROSIE *silently clocks this information.* EDITH *realises what she's revealed.*

I don't know why I said that.

ROSIE: It's okay, this is what happens with my brides. They tell me everything.

EDITH: It just flew out of me.

ROSIE: You'd be surprised how much personal disclosure goes down when you're this close to someone's face.

EDITH: You are *right there.*

ROSIE: What happens in the makeup chair, stays in the makeup chair.

EDITH: Thanks.

ROSIE: So your father had affairs?

EDITH: … Yes.

ROSIE: Even though he was married.

EDITH: Yes.

ROSIE: And Prime Minister.

EDITH: Yes.

ROSIE: And your mum never knew?

EDITH: Mum knew.

ROSIE: *Your mum knew?*

EDITH: It was a 'thing'.

ROSIE: A 'thing'?

EDITH: You know, a whole 'don't ask don't tell' thing.

ROSIE: Hello Daddy.

EDITH: No, it wasn't *anything* like that.

ROSIE: Sounds like it was a little bit like that.

EDITH: No it wasn't. He travelled. A lot. The men in his circles do far worse when they travel. And sometimes when he travelled, that's who he would take. That was the arrangement.

ROSIE: So much for the family man.

EDITH: He was a family man.

> ROSIE *makes a face.*

There was a version of him that was a family man.

> ROSIE *makes a face.*

What?

ROSIE: Nothing!

EDITH: You made a face.

ROSIE: That's just my face sometimes.

EDITH: A family man is the image I need to preserve. It's what he would have wanted.

ROSIE: Sounds a bit like what you want as well.

EDITH: If I don't maintain that, it reflects on me.

ROSIE: So it *benefits* you.

EDITH: What?

ROSIE: Playing happy family benefits you. Just own it.

EDITH: … I was his prop.

ROSIE: And now he's yours.

EDITH: No.

ROSIE: You're using his death that way.

EDITH: I was his prop, why shouldn't he be mine?

> *Pause.*

Dad was with Celeste the night he died. Not with us.

ROSIE: Right.

EDITH: In his last few months he decided what mattered to him, and it wasn't me and Mum.

ROSIE: So no Monopoly then?

EDITH: No Monopoly.

ROSIE: … You made a whole thing about winning.

EDITH: I did.

ROSIE: So none of that was true?

EDITH: I am very good at Monopoly.

ROSIE: You like *corrected me* on it.

EDITH: That's the story we're running with.

ROSIE: But why tell a whole story about it?

EDITH: Come on, Rosie. Your authentic real-girl naivety is getting boring.

ROSIE: Well I'm finding it hard to keep up with all the lies.

EDITH: Everyone lies. *Everyone.* Behind every beautiful success story are ugly machinations.

ROSIE: But why isn't the truth enough?

EDITH: Because the truth is I had Dad's security detail help move him home. His body. Discreetly. So no-one would know. So I could run in his seat.

Beat.

You think I'm gonna win telling that story?

Pause.

I told him that if anything happened, I was ready. He said, 'I'm not dead yet and you're already planning a takeover?' We didn't speak for weeks. He rang me—*he never rings*—so I think it's an apology. And I take the call, but it's Celeste.

'Your father's died. So how do you want this to go?'

So this is it. Not the succession I imagined.

Mum and I agree. We need him at home, in bed, in his pyjamas.

I told Celeste what was going to happen and she was distraught.

And I thought, 'This is my father who just died. Hold yourself together. Have some respect.'

I call his security escort. They arranged moving Dad home. Discreetly. No sirens. No motorcade.

I couldn't look at his face. His lips were thinner. His cheeks sunken. His skin looked strange.

It wasn't him.

Mum comes in wearing her nightgown and slips into bed. She tells me I should spend the night too. Together as a family.

So I sat awake on the armchair next to their bed.

And the next morning we called the coroner.

ROSIE: ... *That's a lot.*

EDITH: We went all out for the wake. Bottomless Dom Perignon. Mum said we were going to throw a party worthy of the occasion. Don't give anyone a reason to think his family didn't love him. 100K event. The alcohol alone came to 62K.

ROSIE: That is just so extra. Your life is like a full-blown telenovela.

EDITH: Cliché?

ROSIE: Melodramatic. I mean, my family has drama, but your family has melodrama.

EDITH: What's the difference?

ROSIE: Money.

Pause.

EDITH: Don't repeat that to anyone.

ROSIE: 62K on alcohol.

EDITH: ...

ROSIE: 62K would pretty much solve all my problems.

EDITH: ...

ROSIE: ... I said 62K would pretty much solve my problems.

EDITH: Just stating facts?

ROSIE: ...

EDITH: Or were you ... ?

ROSIE: Was I what?

EDITH: ...

ROSIE: ...

EDITH: The information you're privileged to in this room requires a level of professionalism.

ROSIE: Well you're just gabbing away like I'm part of the furniture.

EDITH: What?

ROSIE: I'm here, at work, and you're dropping all your state secrets like I'm not even a person worth worrying about.

EDITH: Oh, no, no I wasn't.

ROSIE *gives her a look, 'No?'*

Rosie, that's not how I see it.

ROSIE: You would never be so sloppy if I were important enough.

EDITH: So what are you asking for?

ROSIE: …

EDITH: You want me to *compensate* you for your discretion?

ROSIE: What?

EDITH: Isn't that what you're getting at?

ROSIE: You think I'm blackmailing you?

EDITH: It's pretty close territory.

ROSIE: You think I have no integrity at all?

EDITH: Well you clearly need the money.

ROSIE: *Excuse you?*

EDITH: …

ROSIE: …

EDITH: Look, I think we're having a misunderstanding. And I apologise for that.

ROSIE: What am I worth to you?

EDITH: Listen, I'm not willing to misuse public funds.

ROSIE: From what I've learned in this room today, I think that's bullshit.

EDITH: I felt comfortable with you and I disclosed private information so now—

ROSIE: What's it worth to the tabloids?

EDITH: It'll get you two grand. Three tops.

ROSIE: That might not sound like much to you.

EDITH: But then again, you signed an NDA.

ROSIE: I'm well aware.

EDITH: And if you breach it, someone in my legal team—

ROSIE: [*sarcasm*] Oh no, not the lawyers.

EDITH: They'll destroy you.

ROSIE: If you tell them it was me.

EDITH: They'd work it out. They're very good at what they do.

ROSIE *glances around the room, her eyes rest on the garment rack.*

ROSIE: You could give me the Chanel.

EDITH: That is a fifteen-thousand-dollar dress.

ROSIE: *What?*

EDITH: That dress cost fifteen thousand dollars.

ROSIE: Sold.

EDITH: But that's my dress.

ROSIE: You're not even wearing it today.

EDITH: It's one of my back-up dresses and I intend on wearing it a different day.

ROSIE: Well … if I'm the last one out of the room … and your dress goes missing …

EDITH: Hotel management will call the police.

ROSIE: And I'll just blame it on housekeeping.

EDITH: How feminist of you.

ROSIE: Because housekeepers are all women?

EDITH: *What is this?* What are you doing right now? You're not gonna steal from me.

ROSIE: I could though.

EDITH: We both know you won't.

ROSIE: Do we?

EDITH: So you are threatening me.

ROSIE: …

EDITH: Can you stomach undermining one of the most significant moments for women in this country?

ROSIE: I'm desperate, aren't I?

EDITH: Everything we've worked for: gone.

ROSIE: So then give me the fucking dress!

EDITH: Do not raise your voice at me.

ROSIE: You didn't even pay for it!

EDITH: I earned it though.

ROSIE: See! That! *That right there.*

EDITH: What?

ROSIE: Entitlement!

EDITH: Entitlement? You're the one acting like the gap between us *entitles you* to grab a gift bag on the way out.

ROSIE: You get free stuff, why shouldn't I?

EDITH: And what's a dress going to solve? Your debt isn't about money, it's about behaviour. It's about choices. And if you want your life to look different, you need to make better choices.

ROSIE: Well some people don't have access to those kinds of choices.

EDITH: Oh, grow up. Your hot-mess persona is as much of a performance as anything I'm doing. Because that way you don't have to grab ahold of any power you have and do something with it.

ROSIE: I don't have that kind of power!

EDITH: Well you only get power if you know how to use it.

ROSIE: SO WHY DON'T I USE WHAT I HAVE AND TELL EVERYONE YOUR SECRETS?!

EDITH laughs, this is hilarious to her, it disarms ROSIE.

EDITH: Trust me, this—*whatever this is*—isn't in your best interests.

Beat.

You want to destroy me, Rosie?

ROSIE *struggles, she can't find the words.*

Do you think destroying me is in your interest?

ROSIE *doesn't know anymore.*

I promise you, I'm a much better option. Me, being who I am, means something. People love me.

ROSIE: They don't actually love 'you' though, they love the idea of you.

EDITH: This is happening. Like you said, I've been laying low in the shadows, and now it's my time to shine. And you promised me that with your powers you were going to help me walk out that door and absolutely slay today. So I suggest you pick up that highlighter palette and make me sparkle.

ROSIE *doesn't concede.*

Silence.

EDITH *sits in her self-disgust.*

She can't look at her speech now. Holding it is making her deeply uncomfortable.

Then unable to bear it any longer, EDITH *stands up, walks to the same bin the flowers are in and dumps the speech in there with them.*

She looks back at the makeup chair, terrified of going out there.

So what's that, ah, {twelve minutes}.

EDITH *sits back in the chair and starts to style her own hair. It's kind of cringey to watch.*

ROSIE *lets* EDITH *attempt to finish the pony for a moment. But watching* EDITH *destroy her hard work becomes unbearable.*

ROSIE: We can still make it.

EDITH: …

ROSIE: I'm very fucking good at what I do.

EDITH *nods to* ROSIE *to say, 'Alright, keep going.'*

EDITH *puts down the hairbrush.* ROSIE *springs into action.*

At moments, ROSIE *passes the hair straightener to* EDITH *to hold when she needs two hands.* EDITH *holds the straightener, the brush, the hairpins at various moments. It's a seamless connection.*

Edith's phone buzzes.

[*Looking at the screen*] It's your mum.

EDITH: [*the passcode*] One two three four.

ROSIE: [*typing the passcode*] Tight security.

[*Reading the message*] Link to a news site.

[*Looking at the screen*] Oh wait—green dots—she's typing.

It buzzes again.

It says, 'Have you seen this?'

EDITH: Which news site?

ROSIE: *Daily Telegraph.*

EDITH: Tabloids. Probably a cartoon of me fucking an animal.

ROSIE: Ouch.

EDITH: 'Political satire.' Depicting me as Lilith: a she-demon.

ROSIE: Green dots.

EDITH: They completely missed the literary reference. Pasiphaë fucked a bull, not Lillith. More embarrassing for them really.

It buzzes again.

ROSIE: Your mum says, 'Is this true?'

EDITH: Open it.

ROSIE: Posted at {six forty-one a.m.}. {Seven minutes} ago. [*Reading*] 'NEW PM's Marriage Breakdown. Mr Adam Reynolds, husband to incoming Prime Minister Ms Edith Aldridge, will not be attending the swearing in ceremony today, sparking further rumours that the pair are in the process of a divorce after a source close to the family confirmed Mr Reynolds initiated divorce proceedings in July before Ms Aldridge's campaign was announced. *The Telegraph* reached out to the couple who declined to comment.'

Pause.

Why would they write that?

EDITH: Because they're tabloids.

Edith's phone rings.

ROSIE: [*looking at the screen*] It's your mum.

EDITH *takes the call.*

EDITH: [*on the phone*] Mum?

No, it's nothing, it's tabloids.

It's character assassination.

No, it's crap. You and Dad went through the same shit.

Well no Adam won't be at the ceremony because the plane's grounded.

I didn't tell you because there is NOTHING I can do about the fog in Melbourne.

I DON'T KNOW WHAT YOU WANT ME TO DO, MUM, THE PLANES ARE LITERALLY GROUNDED.

No don't speak to the press, you haven't been prepped.

You haven't been prepped!

Look, I have to go. I have to get dressed and be downstairs in {twelve minutes}.

I'll see you on the lawns.

DON'T WEAR ANYTHING FLORAL.

EDITH *hangs up.*

ROSIE: You're getting clammy again.

EDITH: Tasha needs to find out what happened—who said what to whom—and shut it down.

ROSIE: Look up for a second.

EDITH: There is no upside.

ROSIE: No, look up so I can fix your mascara.

EDITH: Oh.

ROSIE: Let's switch to waterproof.

EDITH: Why waterproof? You think I'm gonna cry today?

ROSIE: You could if you wanted to.

EDITH: I'm definitely not going to cry.

> *Edith's phone rings. It's Tasha.* EDITH *takes the phone from* ROSIE *and answers.*

[*On the phone*] Tasha! How quickly can we bury this? Sue those fuckers. Have legals look into it … And while you're dealing with that, I'll just write a statement and finesse my speech and achieve complexion perfection in the next {ten minutes}? … I haven't spoken with Adam yet, but I imagine he'll be— No, don't worry about Adam, I'll deal with Adam.

> EDITH *hangs up the phone.*

> *Long pause.*

ROSIE: You okay?

EDITH: Just have to decide in the next {ten minutes} or so if I want a divorce.

ROSIE: Adam wants a divorce?

EDITH: I do. But it doesn't make sense to go through with it.

ROSIE: Because you love him?

EDITH: Because of how it looks.

ROSIE: I don't think getting a divorce looks like anything.

EDITH: Can't keep a marriage happy. I must be too focused on my career, too ambitious, difficult to be around, a real bitch. 'There's just something I don't like about her.'

ROSIE: I think it's something people would be into.

EDITH: A clickbait circus.

ROSIE: [*realising*] It's totally modern, actually. Just #leaveyourhusband while running a *literal country*? What an *iconic* move. You need a man who ruins your lipstick, not your mascara.

EDITH: It's too messy.

ROSIE: Give them the mess. The pain. All of it. You may as well use it to say something.

EDITH: And what does the mess say?

ROSIE: On the best days of your life there's going to be disappointment. And on the worst days, there can be opportunity. That's truthful for you. [*Beat*] And you should definitely wear the Chanel if you're about to up and leave your husband today.

Edith's phone buzzes. It's Tasha.

EDITH: [*reading the screen*] It's Tasha. The press want a statement.

ROSIE: So give them a statement.

EDITH: And that would be?

ROSIE: [*working through it*] Things change. You're grieving. You're under a lot of pressure. Admit you can't make all of the pieces work all of the time. It's honest and totally human. People will love you for it.

EDITH: [*while texting*] *Well*, the truth is I'm not technically leaving him. We were already separated, but got back together for the campaign.

ROSIE: *What?*

EDITH: *What?*

ROSIE: What do you mean 'got back together for the campaign'?

EDITH: It wasn't working. Someone was always sacrificing. There wasn't space in the relationship for both of our ambitions. We ended things. We kept it quiet. But then Dad was diagnosed. And Adam approached me and said, 'If you're serious about winning, staying married would signal stability. It'll play right into the legacy narrative.' He had a few of his own demands which I was agreeable to. And that was that. [*Beat*] Wow! That felt good to tell the truth.

ROSIE: Oh no, you can never repeat that.

EDITH: Repeat what?

ROSIE: No, that is way way too much.

EDITH: Too much what?

ROSIE: Truth!

EDITH: You said tell the truth.

ROSIE: When it was an empowering act of self-acceptance, not a calculated part of the PR machine.

EDITH: I'm starting to detect a tone of judgement in your voice and I'm in the makeup chair which is supposed to be a safe space.

ROSIE: People will hate you if they find that out.

EDITH: So what do I do?

ROSIE: LIE!

> *Edith's phone rings. It's Adam.*

EDITH: It's Adam.

ROSIE: Look. Spin what you have to spin. But you need to decide what you're willing to be hated over and what you hope to be loved for. That's power.

> EDITH *takes the call.*

EDITH: [*on the phone*] Adam.

ROSIE: Hair's done! I just need hairspray.

> ROSIE *passes the straightener to* EDITH, *as* EDITH *takes the call from Adam. At some point, perhaps immediately,* EDITH *sets down the straightener. Or perhaps it's not clear who sets it down.*

EDITH: [*on the phone*] We're holding it together, Rosie and I.
  The makeup girl—ah, artist.
  Tasha needs me to make a statement.
  She doesn't know specifics, but yes she does know some details.
  Adam?
  It's safe to assume the whole team knows those details.
  Well as my advisor, I don't think your advice was watertight.
  Uh-huh.
  We can stick with the plan. Or I can change the conversation.
  … Uh-huh.

> EDITH *hangs up the phone.*

ROSIE: Close your eyes.

> ROSIE *mists* EDITH*'s hair with hairspray.*

> EDITH *smells something burning.*

And open.

EDITH: What's that smell?

ROSIE: Yeah something does smell a bit—?

EDITH: Sort of plasticky?

ROSIE: [*realising what it is*] OH MY GOD.

EDITH: What?

ROSIE: OH SHITTTTTTT! No no no no / no no no no—

EDITH: What is it?

ROSIE: FUCK, how bad did it burn—?

EDITH: What's BURNING?

ROSIE: [*discovering the extent of the damage*] Oh my God!

EDITH: Is something on fire?

> ROSIE *holds up* EDITH*'s orange dress, which has been badly singed by the hair straightener.*

Oh my God!

ROSIE: …

EDITH: Tell me it's fixable.

ROSIE: I don't know.

EDITH: Tell me I can still wear it.

ROSIE: I don't know!

EDITH: You did this on purpose!

ROSIE: No, I put the hair straightener down—

EDITH: I thought we agreed on SOFT CURLS.

ROSIE: We did!

EDITH: Then why is there a STRAIGHTENER in sight?

ROSIE: You use a STRAIGHTENER to curl your hair, Edith, not a CURLER!

> EDITH *takes the dress from* ROSIE.
>
> *She surveys the damage.*

EDITH: Can you clean the mark off?

ROSIE: I don't know! I don't think so.

EDITH: I can still wear it. We need to call housekeeping and get this fixed. YOU need to FIX it while I work on my speech.

ROSIE: I can't. It's not fixable.

EDITH: Well THAT is the dress I'm wearing so FIX it.

ROSIE: Edith, listen—

EDITH: This dress you've ruined—

ROSIE: I didn't!

EDITH: Costs more than you make in a year.

ROSIE: I'm sorry!

EDITH: …

ROSIE: …

EDITH: …

ROSIE: [*very tentatively*] Can you wear one of your back-up dresses?

EDITH: This is a back-up dress.

ROSIE: Can you wear one of the other back-up dresses?

EDITH: They're terrible. I would never wear those.

ROSIE: Then why call them back-ups if you don't plan on using them as back-up?

EDITH: It's just what's done.

ROSIE: That makes NO SENSE.

EDITH: Well I've never needed this many back-up dresses in ONE DAY.

ROSIE: I SAID I WAS SORRY. If this is such a big deal then someone way way way more senior than me should have been in charge and whoever that is should probably get fired now because this is a really shitty situation they've put us in because everything you own costs a lot of money! Like probably way more than the limit on most credit cards when you earn twenty thousand a year—

EDITH: Rosie, stop—

ROSIE: I'M TRYING TO DRAG MYSELF OUT OF THIS HELL but I guess one mistake can destroy you!

EDITH: Rosie, STOP!

> EDITH *leads* ROSIE *to the couch.*

You're fine. You're alright.

> *They sit together while* ROSIE *catches her breath.*
>
> EDITH*'s stomach fills with dead.*
>
> EDITH *checks the time.*

{Six fifty-six.}

ROSIE: Not long now.

EDITH: …

ROSIE: Big moment for you.

EDITH: …

ROSIE: This is normally where I tell my brides to take it all in, because moments like this can pass so quickly, and then you look back and realise at the exact best moment of the day you were busy worrying about some insignificant detail.

EDITH: [*suddenly angry*] Can you stop TALKING?! Stop giving your opinion on everything! I need to hear MYSELF think right now.

EDITH *stands and finds a hotel notepad. Then rejoins* ROSIE *on the couch.*

I need a pen.

EDITH *again stands to walk to the other side of the room to get a pen for herself, then rejoins* ROSIE *once more.*

EDITH *writes silently on the hotel notepad.*

The hotel phone begins to ring. ROSIE *moves to answer it.*

Leave it. Let it ring.

The phone rings out.

ROSIE *gets up and begins to pack up her things.*

ROSIE *goes to leave.*

Stay.

Beat as ROSIE *absorbs this. There is an awareness between the two women that something profound has built between them since* ROSIE *walked in the door.*

EDITH *picks up the magazine. She looks at her face on the cover.*

So that's that then. I guess I'll just walk out there with nothing to wear, and no husband by my side, and no team waiting in the wings. Just head on out there with no armour. Completely fucking naked.

ROSIE *goes to get her backpack. She pulls out the jumpsuit she was going to wear to Johnny's birthday dinner.*

ROSIE: Try it on.

EDITH *accepts the invitation. She puts on the jumpsuit. The shoes.* ROSIE *hands her a jacket. She looks sensational.*

We need lipstick.

EDITH: Stone fruit.

ROSIE *applies* EDITH*'s lipstick.*

EDITH *looks in the mirror. She takes in her reflection.*

Rosie's phone rings, the obnoxious ringtone again, it's Johnny.

ROSIE *blocks the call.*

Beat.

ROSIE: You'll need hair and makeup for the formal functions. Full face. Full glam. My choice on dress. Plus touch-ups throughout the evening.

EDITH: You'll need something to wear too.

ROSIE: I'll work something out.

EDITH: Take the dress. The pink one, if you like? It suits you.

> ROSIE *moves to look at the garment bags.*

> EDITH *leaves.*

> ROSIE *turns to wish Edith luck, but she is gone.*

> *Final image of* ROSIE.

> ROSIE *turns on the monitor in the room that shows the stage where* EDITH *will be giving her address.*

> ROSIE *changes into the Chanel.*

> *She applies her own lipstick in the mirror.*

> *She takes in her reflection.*

> EDITH *appears on the monitor, about to speak the first words of her speech.*

> *Both women inhale.*

THE END

RED STITCH | THE ACTORS' THEATRE

presents

Monument

9 AUGUST – 3 SEPTEMBER, 2023

Playwright
Emily Sheehan

Director
Ella Caldwell

Set and Costume Design
Sophie Woodward

Lighting Design
Amelia Lever-Davidson

Sound Design
Danni A. Esposito

Assistant Director
Ibrahim Halaçoglu

Stage Manager
Rain Iyahen

Assistant Stage Manager
Eliza Stone

Makeup Advisor
Harriet O'Donnell

VCA Set and Costume Design Intern
Filipe Filihia

Edith – **Sarah Sutherland**
Rosie – **Julia Hanna**

This play was developed through Red Stitch's INK writing program.

RED STITCH | THE ACTORS' THEATRE

Artistic Director
Ella Caldwell

Interim General Manager
Jennifer Barry

Production Manager
David Bowyer

Front-of-House Manager
Penelope Thomson

Finance
Retinue Accounting

Marketing and Development Coordinators
Darcy Kent and David Whiteley

Administrator
Cecelia Scarthy

RED STITCH ENSEMBLE

Ella Caldwell	Chanella Macri
Richard Cawthorne	Olga Makeeva
Jing-Xuan Chan	Dion Mills
Jessica Clarke	Georgina Naidu
Kate Cole	Christina O'Neill
Brett Cousins	Joe Petruzzi
Ngaire Dawn Fair	Dushan Philips
Daniel Frederikson	Tim Potter
Emily Goddard	Ben Prendergast
Kevin Hofbauer	Kat Stewart
Justin Hosking	Sarah Sutherland
Khisraw Jones-Shukoor	Andrea Swifte
Darcy Kent	David Whiteley
Caroline Lee	Harvey Zielinski

BOARD

Sophia Hall (Chair), Damon Healey (Treasurer), Henrietta Thomas (Secretary), Ella Caldwell, Catherine Cardinet, Humphrey Clegg, Andrew Domasevicius-Zilinskas, Belinda Locke, Michael Rich, and Sandra Willis.

We at Red Stitch acknowledge and pay our respects to Australia's First Peoples and Elders past and present, and offer our gratitude to the Boon Wurrung and Wurundjeri Woi Wurrung peoples of the Kulin Nation, on whose unceded lands we work.

THANK YOU

This development and production of *Monument* would not have been possible without the generous support of our donors and partners

KINDRED DONORS

Jane & Stephen Hains & Portland House Foundation
The Lionel & Yvonne Spencer Trust
Maureen Wheeler AO & Tony Wheeler AO
Lyngala Foundation
Andrew Domasevicius & Aida Tuciute
Carrillo Gantner AC & ZiYin Gantner AC
The James Family Charitable Foundation
Jane Hansen AO
Peter Bartholomew
John Haasz
Graham & Judy Hubbard
Abraham James
Anthony Adair
Michal Alfasi
Beth Brown
Per & Ingrid Carlsen
Simone Clancy
Brian Goddard in Memoriam
The Neff Family
Rosemary Walls
Caitlin English
Linda Herd
Michael Kingston
Caroline Lee
Alex Lewenberg
The Kate & Stephen Shelmerdine Family Foundation
Jane Thompson & Chris Coombs
Christina Turner
Tony Ward & Gail Ryan

Rear 2 Chapel Street, St Kilda East, VIC 3183
http://redstitch.net/ | FB: @RedStitchTheatre | T: @redstitch
boxoffice@redstitch.net | 03 9533 8083

WRITER'S NOTE

Monument is a play about a world leader and her makeup artist and that uniquely intimate relationship. Before I'd written a word of dialogue, I had a very clear stage image in mind of an extraordinary woman having her makeup done. And I knew I wanted audiences to watch this in real time over ninety minutes.

We so often correlate beauty with competence. So to participate in beauty culture is non-negotiable if you're in the public eye. Conversely, hyper-feminine spaces are often seen as unserious, and so with this play I wanted to use the intimacy of the makeup chair as a space capable of anchoring a global, political narrative.

I'm excited to bring Red Stitch audiences this Trojan horse of a play. A play that's easy on the eyes, at first, because the packaging matters. A play that is on the surface is about makeup, image and persona. But as the play goes along, we explore the blurring line between the role of a politician and the influence of a celebrity. What are the ethical dilemmas present in this fusion? As I began writing and researching, inspiration revealed itself as I leaned into this phenomenon.

While listening to Hillary Clinton's autobiography I hear her say that during the 2016 presidential campaign she spent 600 hours getting hair and makeup done. The equivalent of 25 days. And that's just during the campaign.

A statue of Princess Diana is unveiled to mark what would have been her 60th birthday. Twitter is ablaze with critics slamming the statue's outfit as ugly and outdated. This is a statue they're talking about.

At a Christmas party, a woman tells me she trains hairdressers to respond to disclosures of family violence. In fact, a large number of programs have emerged in Australia like this one, as research has consistently found that hair salons are unique spaces of what they call 'touch and talk'.

As New Zealand prepares for lockdown, Prime Minister Jacinda Ardern goes live on Facebook from her bedroom, wearing a well-worn sweatshirt and no-makeup makeup. A defining moment, to be sure. But why?

Alexandria Ocasio-Cortez makes history as the youngest woman elected to US Congress. A fan on Twitter asks what lipstick she was wearing during the debate. She tweets back. It's Stila Stay All Day Liquid in Beso. It sells out at Sephora the same week.

This play is curious about why people say, 'I don't really

follow the news', or 'I don't think that much about what I wear', or 'I don't find politics very interesting'. If you've ever divulged a dark secret or the latest family drama to your hairdresser, then you will understand what this play is getting at.

Thank you to the artistic team Ella Caldwell, Sarah Sutherland, Julia Hanna, Sophie Woodward, Amelia Lever-Davidson, Danni Esposito, Ibrahim Halacoglu and Harriet O'Donnel. Your vision for this play has broadened the horizons of what was possible. Thank you also to Joanna Murray Smith, Laura Tingle, Bridgit Balodis, Tahlee Fereday, Tom Healey and the Red Stitch ensemble for their advice and input in the dramaturgical wrangling of this play.

I hope audiences feel empowered to take the play as seriously as they might take selecting the perfect shade of lipstick. That it is frivolous, of course, and hopefully fun, but at the same time worthy of serious discussion and capable of withstanding meaningful critique. Whether you prefer to express yourself through words, or aesthetics, or art and metaphor, it's between these two poles (frivolity and seriousness) that many meaningful insights in life and in art might be uncovered.

Emily Sheehan

EMILY SHEEHAN
PLAYWRIGHT

Emily Sheehan is a playwright and dramaturg. She completed her master's in playwriting at the Victoria College of Arts. Her plays include *Monument* (Red Stitch Actors' Theatre), *Hell's Canyon* (Old 505 Theatre / La Mama Theatre / Regional Arts Victoria / Vimeo on Demand film of stage play), *Daisy Moon Was Born This Way* (Q Theatre) and *Versions of Us* (Canberra Youth Theatre). Her plays have been developed through Melbourne Theatre Company Cybec, Red Stitch INK, Playwriting Australia National Script Workshops, Playwriting Australia National Play Festival and New Ghosts Theatre Company. Playwriting awards include the Rodney Seaborn Playwrights' Award (Winner), The Patrick White Playwrights' Award (Shortlist), Max Afford Playwrights' Award (Shortlist), UK's Theatre503 Playwriting Award (Longlist) and Melbourne Fringe Festival Award (Winner). Emily has completed dramaturgy attachments with The Bush Theatre (London), Traverse Theatre (Edinburgh) and Playwrights' Studio Scotland and worked as a dramaturg for Theatre503 (London), Arts Centre Melbourne and the Victorian College of the Arts. She has also undertaken dramaturgy observations with the National Theatre of Scotland and Melbourne Theatre Company, and worked as a script reader for Playwriting Australia and Currency Press. Emily teaches playwriting at the Victorian College of the Arts and hosts the Playwright's Process Podcast, a monthly podcast about writing, craft and the creative process.

ELLA CALDWELL
DIRECTOR

Ella is a theatre director and actor. She studied Creative Arts at the University of Melbourne. She is a founding member of Red Stitch Actors' Theatre and has been Artistic Director of the company since July 2013. During this time, Ella has steered the company's new writing program, INK, which has produced numerous acclaimed productions, touring nationally and internationally. Ella also established *PLAYlist*, a biennial site-specific festival of music and new writing. Most recently, Ella directed the critically acclaimed Australian premiere season of Ella Hickson's *Oil*. In 2018 Ella directed *The Antipodes* by Annie Baker, which was included in *Time Out*'s top ten shows of the year. Previous directorial work includes the sold-out Victorian premiere season of Joanna Murray-Smith's *Fury* and the Australian premiere production of *Incognito* by Nick Payne, both directed in collaboration with ensemble member Brett Cousins, and the world premiere of Caleb Lewis' *The Honeybees*. Ella also directed *Watching*, an audio play by Vidya Rajan and Morgan Rose, which featured 18 actors.

As an actor, Ella stepped in to perform the role of Rosemary in the 2022 world premiere season of Morgan Rose's *Fast Food*, directed by Bridget Balodis. Previously, Ella featured in Rose's *desert, 6:29pm*, also directed by Balodis. *desert, 629pm* went on to a sold-out season at Wuzhen Theatre Festival in China on the company's first international tour. Previous acting credits include *The Realistic Joneses* by Will Eno, *The Village Bike* by Penelope Skinner, *Love, Love, Love* by Mike Bartlett, *Midsummer—A Play with Songs* by David Greig and Gordon McIntyre, *Oh Well Never Mind Bye* by Stephen Lally, *The Laramie Project—10 Years Later* by Moises Kaufman, *Stop.Rewind* by Melissa Bubnic, *The Winterling* by Jez Butterworth, *Crestfall* by Mark O'Rowe, *Outlying Islands* by David Greig, *The Night Season* by Rebecca Lenkiewicz and *Bug* by Tracy Letts.

SOPHIE WOODWARD
SET AND COSTUME DESIGN

Sophie is a Melbourne-based set and costume designer. Sophie graduated with a Bachelor of Production (Design) from VCA in 2010 winning the Beleura John Tallis Design Award in her final year. Sophie recently designed costumes for Melbourne Theatre Company's *Come Rain or Come Shine*. Recent set and costume designs include *A Simple Act of Kindness* (Red Stitch Actors Theatre) and *All the Shining Lights* (HotHouse Theatre). Earlier design work from Sophie includes *Hungry Ghosts* (Melbourne Theatre Company); *Burn This*, *The One* and *Mr Burns, A Post Electric Play* (fortyfivedownstairs); *Those Who Fall in Love like Anchors Dropped Upon the Ocean Floor*, *Between the Clouds*, *Pyjama Girl* and *Letters from the Border* (HotHouse Theatre); *Fast Food*, *Iphigenia in Splott*, *Grace*, *Extinction*, *Rules for Living*, *You Got Older*, *The Honey Bees*, *The Village Bike*, *Wet House*, *Love Love Love*, *4,000 Miles* and *Day One. A Hotel, Evening* (Red Stitch Actors' Theatre); *#No Exemptions*, *Thigh Gap* and *A Long Day's Dying* (LaMama Theatre). Sophie was Costume Design Associate on *Girls & Boys*, *Bernhardt/Hamlet*, *An Ideal Husband* and *Twelfth Night* (Melbourne Theatre Company).

AMELIA LEVER-DAVIDSON
LIGHTING DESIGN

Amelia Lever-Davidson is an award-winning lighting designer for theatre, dance, live art, installation and events. Amelia is a graduate of The Victorian College of the Arts, The Western Australian Academy of the Performing Arts and RMIT. Amelia has designed lighting for Sydney Theatre Company, Melbourne Theatre Company, Belvoir St Theatre, Malthouse Theatre, RISING Festival, DARK MOFO, Chunky Move, Red Stitch, Chamber Made, Circa, Elbow Room, Belarus Free Theatre, Deep Soulful Sweats, The Hayloft Project, MKA, and many others. She has collaborated with a diverse range of directors and choreographers, and her work has been presented both nationally and internationally. Amelia has also worked as a lighting director for Melbourne International Comedy Festival (Special Events), Channel Ten, Channel Nine, and the ABC. Amelia's work has been recognised with Green Room Awards for multiple works. Amelia is an Australia Council ArtStart and JUMP Mentorship recipient, Ian Potter Cultural Trust recipient, a past participant in the Malthouse Besen Family Artist Program and the Melbourne Theatre Company's inaugural Women in Theatre Program.

DANNI A. ESPOSITO
SOUND DESIGN

Danni is a trans non-binary composer and sound designer from Naarm, working across theatre and film. They are a recent graduate of Victorian College of the Arts and hold a Bachelor of Fine Arts in Production. Danni's credits include: as composer and sound designer: for Bighouse Arts: *Tram Lights Up*; for Griffin Theatre Company: *Sex Magick*; *Slut*; for Darebin Arts: *Hydra*; for Darlinghurst Theatre Company: *Overflow*; for Essential Theatre: *The Dream Laboratory*; for Fever103 Theatre: *Treats* and *Brittany and The Mannequins*; for La Mama: *Cactus*; for Malthouse Theatre/Darlinghurst Theatre Company: *Stay Woke*; for Midsumma Festival: *Adam, Guerilla Sabbath, Slutnik*; for Melbourne Writers Festival: *Never Said Motel*; for New Theatricals: *Darkness*; for Patalog Theatre: *Punk Rock*; for Red Stitch: *Fast Food*; for Three Fates Theatre Company: *Land*. Their credits as sound designer include: for Melbourne Theatre Company: *The Sound Inside*; and as assistant sound designer: for Melbourne Theatre Company: *Sunday*. Danni was a panel member for the 2022 Green Room Awards. Danni received a Green Room Award nomination for their work on *Hydra*. They were nominated for a Sydney Theatre Award for Best Composer for their work on *Overflow*.

IBRAHIM HALAÇOGLU
STAGE MANAGER / ASSISTANT DIRECTOR

A theatre-maker from Istanbul, Ibrahim's been professionally involved in theatre since 2010 predominantly as a performer, as well as a director, dramaturg, and playwright. He was a very active participant in the alternative theatre movement in Istanbul. A few years ago, he rediscovered theatre through meddah, an ancient form of Turkish/Ottoman storytelling. He developed a passion for revising traditional storytelling techniques to become a 21st-century storyteller. He currently focuses on queering and contemporising the meddah by combining autoethnography with postmodern narratives and metafiction. He truly believes that fiction can be used in art to make more sense of, or even authenticate, reality. He finished his master's degree in directing at the VCA in 2021. He is the 2022 Graduate Director at Red Stitch Actors' Theatre. He also works as a workshop artist at St Martins Youth Arts Centre. Some of his works in Melbourne include: *The Amateurs* (dir. Susie Dee), *Life Changing Show* (by The People), *The Gospel According to Jesus, Queen of Heaven* (dir. Kitan Petkovski), *Very Nice Pot Plants* (dir. Sheridan and Pardy). Current works in development include: *Peacemongers* (as performer and deviser, co-devisers Morgan Rose and Katrina Cornwell), *HOMO FOMO* (as writer and performer, dir. Alyson Campbell), *Where My Accent Comes From* (as writer, director, and performer).

RAIN IYAHEN
STAGE MANAGER

Rain is a freelance Stage Manager and Production Manager born and raised in Spain. She has lived across the UK and the US in the past 10 years, and she relocated to Australia in 2019. Since then, she's been working in Melbourne's theatre scene. Some Stage Manager credits include: Assistant Stage Manager at

Melbourne Theatre Company's production of *Is God Is* (2023); Touring Stage Manager at Critical Stages' production of *Black Sun Blood Moon* (2023); Stage Manager at Victorian Opera's production of Melbourne, *Cheryomushki* (2023); Assistant Stage Manager at Melbourne Theatre Company's production of *Sunday* (2023); Deputy Stage Manager at Essential Theatre's production of *Emilia* (2022); Deputy Stage Manager at Victorian Opera's production of *The Butterfly Lovers* (2022); Touring Stage Manager at Critical Stages' production of *THEM* (2022); Stage Manager at Red Stitch Theatre's production of *Fast Food* (2022), *Grace* (2022), *The Cane* (2021) and *Single Ladies* (2020). Her credits also include: Production Manager at Darebin Speakeasy's production of *Security* (2022); and St Martins Youth's production of *Gene Tree* (2022).

HARRIET O'DONNELL
MAKEUP ADVISOR

Harriet O'Donnell is an award-winning hair and makeup artist based in Melbourne, with a background in performing arts. For 20 years, she's worked her magic in television, film, fashion and photo shoots, working on a wide variety of faces from pop stars to prime ministers. She's currently a senior in-house makeup artist at the ABC, an industry consultant, and also moonlights as a painter, musician and performer.

FELIPE FILIHIA
VCA SET AND COSTUME DESIGN INTERN

Filipe Filihia is a set and costume designer working in Melbourne, who explores their intersectional heritage through experimental design and storytelling. Currently studying at the Victorian College of the Arts, they are hoping to continue their practice of bringing marginalized communities to the forefront of the theatrical world. Their credits include *LELE* (2022) with Western Edge Youth Arts and *Footprints* working with

First Nations choreographer and VCA alum Ngioka Bunda-Heath, as part of the 2022 VCA Dance Grad season, *Alter Kinetic*.

SARAH SUTHERLAND
EDITH

Sarah Sutherland has been a Red Stitch ensemble member for over fifteen years and has worked extensively across theatre, film, and television during that time. Shows with Red Stitch include *A Simple Act of Kindness, Ulster American, Day One. A Hotel. Evening, The Realistic Jones, Faces In the Crowd, The Pain and the Itch, After Miss Julie, That Face, Motortown* and *Fewer Emergencies*. Sarah has performed leading roles for MTC in *Dead Man's Cell Phone* and *The Water Carriers*, and with the Flinders Quartet in *Behind Closed Doors*. Sarah has also toured nationally and internationally with Red Stitch's award-winning plays *Red Sky Morning* and *desert, 6.29 pm*. On television, Sarah is best known for her role as Kareena in *Angry Boys for ABC/BBC/HBO* and for roles in *Miss Fisher's Modern Murder Mysteries, Neighbours, Stingers,* and *Blue Heelers.* Her numerous short film credits include: Tropfest award-winner *In Your Dreams* as well as *The Postman, The Director, When I Go, Carcass, The Cuckoo,* and *The True History of Billy the Kid.* Sarah is the Artistic Director of Rollercoaster Theatre Company, a not-for-profit ensemble of neurodivergent and mixed-ability actors. Over the 16 years she has been working with Rollercoaster she has produced, directed, and devised many productions including the multi-award-winning short film *Comican't.* Sarah is delighted to be returning to the Red Stitch stage, this time as Prime Minister.

JULIA HANNA
ROSIE

Julia completed her Bachelor of Fine Arts (Acting) at the Victorian College of the Arts (VCA) in 2022. Julia began her training at The American Academy of Dramatic Arts (AADA) in New York where she performed in productions including *Five Women* (dir. Pamela Scott), *Dear Friends* (dir. Jim DeMonic) and *The Dancers* (Dir. Susan Pilar). Since returning to Melbourne Julia has performed in *Mocha Is Not Coffee* (dir. Verity Norbury) at Gasworks Theatre and *The Global Citizen* at La Mama Theatre. Julia has also performed in *Beers and Trees* (dir. Lisa Inman) at La Mama Theatre and *Loose Teeth* at La Mama Courthouse (dir. Cassandra Yiannacou). Last year Julia performed in her final productions at VCA including *Tales From The Vienna Woods* (dir. Mark Wilson) and *Slaughterhouse* (dir. Georgina Naidu) and the *The Wolves* (dir. Yoni Prior). Julia is very excited to perform in *Monument* at Red Stitch this year.

RED STITCH ACTORS' THEATRE

Red Stitch is a creative hub, offering scope for artists to make work they are passionate about in a sector where such opportunities are limited. As the ensemble and executives of Red Stitch, we provide a platform where leading practitioners can hone their craft and take risks, and emerging artists can work alongside mid-career and seasoned professionals. We play a vital role in the development and presentation of new Australian works through our INK playwriting program, promoting local voices alongside acclaimed contemporary international work which may not otherwise be seen by local audiences.

www.redstitch.net

Red Stitch would like to thank the following supporters who generously contribute to our INK program.

Australian Government
RISE Fund

CREATIVE VICTORIA

CITY OF PORT PHILLIP

Cybec Foundation

MALCOLM ROBERTSON FOUNDATION

THE PORTLAND HOUSE FOUNDATION

SBW Foundation
SEABORN, BROUGHTON & WALFORD FOUNDATION
Supporting the Performing Arts

PLAYKING FOUNDATION

Lyngala Foundation

COPYRIGHT AGENCY CULTURAL FUND

SIDNEY MYER FUND

Kindred

THE MYER FOUNDATION

www.ingramcontent.com/pod-product-compliance
Lightning Source LLC
Chambersburg PA
CBHW050020090426
42734CB00021B/3354